TIPS
FROM THE
TRENCHES

What others are saying about this book:

"There are no international boundaries when it comes to Professional Services. Brilliant users' guide for Professional Services people."

Adrian Wookey, VP, Service Delivery, McKesson UK

"This is quite simply a 'wisdom book'. It is an essential guide to success in the professional services industry and a great read, to boot!"

Morris Panner, CEO, OpenAir

"Anyone involved with Professional Services knows that there is no single secret to success. This book offers insight on almost every aspect of building and managing a successful professional services organization."

Kevin Bury, Vice President, QuickArrow

"Faced with today's fiercely competitive business environment, every Professional Services Manager will find this valuable. It provides a significant resource for insightful best-practice experience, useful situation-related information, and excellent real-life stories."

Anthony Sperling, Senior Vice President, Advent Software, Inc.

"An outstanding reference book for every area of a Professional Services Organization. I wish I had it 10 years ago. You're always looking for a great idea and this book gives it to you in a real-life practical manner."

Wendy Reed, CEO, InfoMentis, Inc.

TIPS FROM THE TRENCHES

The Collective Wisdom of Over
100 Professional Services Leaders

Mahesh Baxi • Terry Jansen • Joe Longo
Bill Morton • Jeanne Urich
Contributing Editors

Santa Clara, California

Published by PSVillage Press, Santa Clara, CA 95050
www.psvillage.com

Cover Design: KELLY CONNELLY DESIGN + PRINT, San Francisco, CA, and Bookcovers.com
Interior Design: Mahesh Baxi, and Bookcovers.com

First Edition

Tips from the trenches : the collective wisdom of over 100 professional services leaders / Mahesh Baxi ... [et al.], contributing editors.
p. cm.
At head of title: PSVillage.
LCCN 2007931342
ISBN-13: 978-0-9796952-2-3
ISBN-10: 0-9796952-2-8

1. Information technology--Management. 2. Information consultants. 3. Information resources management. I. Baxi, Mahesh. II. PSVillage (Firm) III. Title: PSVillage tips from the trenches

T58.64.T56 2007 658.4'038
QBI07-700133

10 9 8 7 6 5 4 3 2 1

Printed and bound in the United States of America

Dedication

This book is dedicated to the members of the global Professional Services community, who deserve the highest praise for their problem-solving abilities, big hearts, resourcefulness, and tenacity in creating customer and business success.

Acknowledgments

This book would not have been possible without the help and support of so many friends of PSVillage.

First, we'd like to thank our book Sponsors: *OpenAir*, *QuickArrow*, and *InfoMentis, Inc.* for their unwavering dedication and commitment to the Professional Services community and to the publication of this book. Without their financial support, this book would just be one of those ideas that never saw the light of day. We'd also like to thank our advertisers, Project Locker and Unanet Technologies, for their financial support of our book.

We also extend our deepest gratitude to both the Core Team and the Extended Team of Contributing Authors listed below - a very special group of folks who are true standouts in the PS community - for immersing themselves in our book project and helping us bring it to fruition:

Core Team

Mahesh Baxi, Sr. Director, Professional Services
Joe Longo, Vice President Professional Services, MetricStream
Bill Morton, Vice President of Services, Acesis Inc.
Jeanne Urich, Management Consultant, Adexta

Extended Team

Dave Brown, IBM Alliance Leader, Capgemini
Jason Blessing, General Manager, Taleo Business Edition
Scott Fletcher, Director, InfoMentis, Inc.
Jon Harris, Chief Service Officer, Ultimate Software
Beth Martinko, Vice President Services, Wavelight
Carole L. McCluskey, President, EttenAj Consulting LLC

And a very special thanks to all the Contributing Authors who so generously contributed their time, energy and expertise to make this book possible so that others might learn from their experiences.

About PSVillage

PSVillage is an industry-leading, global community of nearly 1000 Technology Professional Services Leaders representing over 450 companies. The only networking forum of its kind, PSVillage was founded in 2004 to provide a forum for Professional Services Leaders to collaborate and share research, best practices, resources and more. The site hosts a moderated discussion forum, an on-line magazine, a niche job board, PS benchmarks and PSA reviews, a spotlight of members and a variety of free or low-cost services including webinars, white papers, workshops, research and networking events. To learn more, go to www.psvillage.com.

Table of Contents

5. Services Marketing 101

6. Services Selling 119

7. Services Delivery 139

8. Offshoring 155

9. Cross-Functional Alignment 171

Letter from the Editor

Creating this book has been a fascinating journey. It started as the seed of an idea over a year ago – the title reverberating in my mind every time I walked my dog, went out for a bike ride or drove in Bay Area commute traffic. It seemed that any spare time I had was consumed by thoughts of what the creation and publication of a book like this could mean for the Professional Services community. Not only would it bring us closer together as a community, but what a terrific resource it would be! So little information exists in the PS arena – where does one go (other than PSVillage, of course!) to learn how others have developed PS strategy, how they're measuring utilization and incenting their consultants, and what techniques they're using in their hiring practices? This book, I concluded, would be a great way to encourage seasoned PS leaders in our community to document and share their experiences.

But coming up with the idea was one thing – actually acting on it was another. How would I get 100 PS leaders to contribute with their busy schedules? On top of that, I knew little about publishing a book and while I was willing to spearhead the project, it would only be successful if I were able to pull together the right team to help me. The team must consist of true PS thought leaders with deep experience in professional services.

And then, not surprisingly, the PS world started to rub off on me. I started to think in terms of metrics – if I had five core team members working with two folks each, and each of the 10 were responsible for bringing in tips from 10 services leaders, we'd have our 100 tips! It was a good formula, I thought, and one that wouldn't put too much of a burden on any one person.

With that plan in mind, I began reaching out to our PSVillage members to ask for their help and was amazed at the receptivity. I know I shouldn't have been amazed – PS folks have some of the biggest hearts and are some of the best problem-solvers on the planet, but I was truly in awe of the willingness of so many people to help get my idea off the ground. Joe Longo, Bill Morton, Mahesh Baxi, and

Jeanne Urich enthusiastically embraced the idea and formed the core team, meeting every Saturday morning for four months straight to complete the book. Beth Martinko, Carole McCluskey, Jason Blessing, Scott Fletcher, Jon Harris and Dave Brown jumped in to help out as the extended team. It was like a well-oiled machine – everyone working together towards deadlines and goals. Friendships were forming, ideas were being exchanged, PS executives were connecting with each other - all in an effort to create the industry's first community-developed book. The end result is nothing short of spectacular.

I'd like to thank everyone who participated in this book – the core team who made the whole process a lot of fun and who were relentless in making target dates and delivering a quality product, the extended team who hustled up tips to hit our target of 100, and all of the contributing authors who spent precious time and effort writing terrific tips that will serve as an inspiration to thousands of services leaders. From armadillo racing to how to get out of Denver in the middle of a blizzard to taking advantage of hotel happy hours for team meetings while on a tight budget, there's a tip in this book for everyone. I hope you find it to be a fun and informative read! I certainly did!

Theresa L. Jansen

Terry Jansen
Founder, PSVillage

About the Editor

Terry Jansen is the founder of PSVillage, an industry-leading, global community of Professional Services Leaders with nearly 1000 members representing some 450 companies. Previously an executive search consultant specializing in Professional Services, Terry launched PSVillage in 2004 after discussing the concept with one hundred PS leaders who embraced the need for this type of community. Prior to her 10 years in the search business, Terry held marketing management and corporate communications positions with Unisys Corporation. Terry holds a Bachelor of Business degree in Marketing from the University of Wisconsin - Eau Claire. When she's not busy dreaming up new ideas and programs for PSVillage, you'll find her throwing rocks for her rock-chasing, fence-climbing, escape-artist dog, Molly.

About the Contributing Editors

Joe Longo is MetricStream's Vice President of Professional Services. Joe has over 20 years experience in the computer industry, working for technology vendors providing mission critical solutions to enterprise customers. During his career, Joe has provided direct consulting expertise to major enterprise customers such as the Federal Reserve Bank, Hong Kong Post, Wells Fargo Bank, MCI, and others. Prior to joining MetricStream, Joe was VP of Professional Services for Selectica, Inc., a contract management software company.

Mr. Longo has a degree in Computer Science from the Royal Melbourne Institute of Technology, and a Post Graduate Diploma in Digital Communications from the Chisholm Institute of Technology. He and his wife have three daughters and live in Saratoga, California, the heart of Silicon Valley.

"When Terry Jansen approached me about this project, my immediate reaction was "what a great idea". I expected this to be a fun project, but when the tips starting rolling in, I was deeply inspired. Here were a collection of notes from professionals in my field that were validating many of my own experiences over the past 15 years in services. It was like finding a SETI signal, not just one, but over 160 of them! And they're all like me: passionate about their work, their customers and their services colleagues. I've also met an extended group of PS professionals who have helped on this book, and every one of them is a person I want to know for a very long time. So it seems I'll be in this field for quite a while. I hope this book will be a valuable reference guide for anyone related to the field of Professional Services, and that you find it as inspiring to read as I have."

Jeanne Urich is a management consultant specializing in service organization improvement for small to large technology companies. Her focus areas include: Strategy, Marketing, Business Development, Alliances, Finance and Operations and Human Resources. She has been a corporate officer and leader of the worldwide services organizations of Vignette, Blue Martini and Clarify. In each of these roles, she led the growth of their Professional Services, Education, Account Management and Alliances organizations and was responsible for dramatically increasing services revenue, profit and utilization while maintaining a balanced relationship with system integration partners. At Clarify, in less than three years, she grew the services organization from 50 to 720 employees and increased annual revenue from $20M to $100M while generating a 24% margin. She has a Bachelor's degree in Math and Computer Science from Vanderbilt University and has completed Executive Programs at Stanford and Brown University.

"Co-editing Tips from the Trenches has been an extremely rewarding experience. I am continually amazed and impressed by the willingness of Professional Services leaders to contribute and help one another. We went from concept to publishing in four months thanks to the overwhelming response from the PSVillage community. With a very tight timeline for "tip submission" we received over 160 invaluable tips. Working with the authors and editors was a dream job – teamwork, cooperation and humor contributed to create a product that was bigger and better than anyone initially imagined. I wish I had had a guide like 'Tips' when I started leading Professional Services organizations. I have read and re-read every tip and immediately started applying the wisdom I gleaned from this amazing book. I hope you will enjoy it and benefit from it as much as I have."

Bill Morton is currently Acesis Inc.'s Vice President of Services. Bill has more than 20 years experience managing Professional Services, Training, and Customer Support organizations for enterprise software companies including Vantive (acquired by PeopleSoft in 2000), Informix, ViewStar, Dorado and Nextance. A special highlight of Bill's career was building the Vantive CRM consulting organization from one person and no revenue to 350 consultants worldwide with an $85 million annual revenue run rate. During eight years under Bill's direction, Vantive's consulting organization delivered more than 1500 successful CRM projects and developed partnering relationships with more than 50 companies in the US, Canada, Europe and Asia. Bill has a Bachelor's and Master's degree in Electrical Engineering from MIT and an MBA from Harvard University.

"I have been involved with Professional Services management for about 25 years, and I am the first to admit that many of those years involved trial and error, re-tooling, re-thinking, and re-treading the techniques I have used in coping with the multitude of nuances and complexities involved in managing the delivery of value-added PS projects to customers all around the world. If I had been provided with more than 150 PS "tips" 25 years ago, my guess is that I would have put many of them to good use, and my trip up the PS learning curve would probably have been substantially accelerated. In reading any book of "tips" most readers will have a mixture of reactions to individual tips. The reactions may range from "I knew that" to "What a silly idea" to "Wow, that makes great sense and I will try it out in my PS organization"! In reading this book, if you have a "Wow" reaction to just a few tips, then this book could have a profound effect on the creativity, enjoyment and success that you and your PS teammates experience in your PS careers."

Mahesh Baxi is Senior Director, Professional Services. With over 14 years of experience in the software industry, Mahesh has extensive experience in executing large enterprise projects with cross-functional and global delivery teams in multiple geographical locations. Mahesh has led CRM and B2B practices and has comprehensive experience in services business development activities. Mahesh holds a Bachelors in Computer Engineering from India.

"Working on this book has been an amazing experience – one that cannot be described in just a few words. I have benefited in ways that will greatly enhance my work in PS, from expanding my network of services leaders to learning how others have solved difficult PS issues, to the satisfaction of publishing a book that will be invaluable to our industry. This book will undoubtedly be a resource that will come in handy throughout the course of my career in services, and one that will be a fixture on my desk. I hope you are as inspired by the collective wisdom of our community as I have been."

Contributing Authors by Name with Tip Numbers

Author Name	Tip Number
Alexander, James A.	3, 13, 42
Alvarez, Aramis	7, 53
Anur, Arun	120
Aune, Glenda	51, 62, 66, 160
Bates, Bob	39
Baxi, Mahesh	46
Bayless, Charles	55
Becker, Gerard F.	25
Begun, Alvin	34, 92
Blessing, Jason	57, 105
Blumenfield, Neil.	153
Boehnlein, Bob	14, 27, 130
Bose, Ashim	5
Brown, Dave	102
Brown, Olga	30, 132
Cappello, Toby	9
Carr, Alex	88
Catbagan, Dan	124
Chen, George	43, 165
Cicci, Jodi	29, 131
Corbin, Daryl	151
Costello, Keith	41, 156
Eicher, Micheal	24, 78
Fauscette, Michael	72, 141
Fawver, Kevin	37
Field, Don	75
Fletcher, Scott	70
Foster, Justin	33
Franco, Nello	36
Freedman, Robert	10
Frenza, JP	90
Giangregorio, Steven	82, 129

1. Strategy and Charter

This chapter covers topics such as services mission and strategy, when to make money, reasons for being, purpose of an organization, charter of a PS organization and strategic alignment.

"My team has created a very innovative solution, but we're still looking for a problem to go with it."

1 Three Eyes for Success

If a PS Manager keeps one eye on customer success, one eye on the training, productivity and career development of PS personnel, and one eye on meeting the oftentimes conflicting needs of Sales, Finance and Product Engineering, then the PS Manager will be successful. Of course, this takes three eyes, but this is merely one more problem-solving exercise for a seasoned PS Executive!

Bill Morton, Vice President of Services, Acesis Inc.

2 Demonstrating the Value of the PS Organization

It can be a challenge for the captive services department to be viewed as a strategic contributor to the core mission of the company. In fact, I have worked for a couple of CEOs who view Professional Services as some kind of necessary evil (unless you have a really stellar quarter, of course)! Sensing this challenge, and recognizing that one of our core company value propositions was the impact our hosted ASP solution had on our customer's business outcomes, we created a strategic practice area within the professional services team. The 'Optimization Services' group specifically focused on demonstrating how usage of our solutions impacted our client's business results. In fact, we offered a free business outcome (ROI) study to clients who generated over a certain amount of annual transaction revenue.

Move the debate about the role of the Professional Services team towards a broader strategic role.

On the face of it, this represented a significant investment of non-billable time and resource (which, frankly, we had been investing in any case, but in a highly reactive way). After we had been doing these studies for a while, we decided to do our own study of the impact our "free" ROI studies had on our own business results. Amazingly, we found that clients for whom we had completed these free studies had subsequently gone on to increase their usage of our hosted transaction services by up to 50%, and on average, by 10%, easily covering the investment of non-billable time and resource.

Coincidentally, our internal study of the impact of this practice area was completed just before the annual executive team offsite to develop the strategic plan for the following year. The results of the ROI study were presented to the rest of the executive team. They were so impressed by the results that expansion of the optimization practice became a cornerstone of the overall company strategy for the following year. We became all about demonstrating value for more clients more quickly! The key point is that we managed to move the debate about the role of the Professional Services team beyond our ability to generate supplemental revenue towards a broader strategic role in supporting the overall mission of the organization - and directly influencing transaction revenue. Now that will make any CEO happy!

Caroline Paxman, SVP Professional Services

3 Starting a PSO

Starting a PSO from zero is a major undertaking. You have to do everything at once—rapidly grow while maintaining the quality of services. The following five tips came from a panel that I moderated of four VPs of PS within product companies:

Do a great job with the customer first. If not, the sales force will abandon you. Everyone is watching your organization under the microscope for the first 90 days. Do what it takes to create some "showcase" accounts.

Put a major focus on defining, finding, and developing a core leadership team. These people may be really hard to find, but they represent about 80 percent of your risk—they are doing the bidding and managing, and they are dealing with the tough issues. You need people who have been there. Of course you will want to tap any existing talent, but you may have to go outside for some core experiences. You may make enough mistakes on the tough situations—you don't need to make mistakes on the easy ones.

Do a great job with the customer first.

Layer in project management, processes and systems right away. Without strong project management, you will quickly find yourself in a death spiral. You need to define common processes early in order to control consistency and generate efficiencies.

Constantly communicate and tell your organization that the best way to build customer relationships is with professional services interactions. If you do this right, you can have customers for life. Get key people in your organization to realize that professional services are a key part of corporate success.

Everybody needs training. Of course they do. You are asking people to do new and different things. Have a training and development plan (and budget) in place from the beginning. Invest in high-quality, professional-services-specific training.

James A. Alexander, Ed.D., Alexander Consulting

4 Listen – and Create your Charter

I've bootstrapped services organizations and I've taken over existing ones. Which is harder? Taking control of an existing organization is certainly the most challenging. My advice to someone in this situation is to spend the first few weeks listening carefully. Listen to your sales organization – meet with the leaders and ask them what they expect from you. Simply schedule a brief meeting with your head of sales and ask "what do you expect of me, and of my organization". She'll tell you. And listen to your services team leads and thought leaders. Ask them about their challenges and what they expect. When you've developed key insights, create a simple charter: why you exist in the bigger scheme, who are your customers, what are your objectives, how you will achieve them. Summarize these points in a simple presentation. Perform a sanity check with your team leads, then present it to the company executives for ratification.

> **Create a frame of reference with your peers and company leadership that will guide you through the challenges ahead.**

You'll get high marks for your team for creating an identity for them. And you'll have created a frame of reference with your peers and company leadership that will guide you through the challenges ahead.

Joe Longo, VP Professional Services, MetricStream

5 Including Services in a Product Company's Strategy

Are you a services executive in a company whose reason for being is selling higher margin hardware or software? How does Professional Services become a part of corporate strategy? How do you prevent you and your team from being relegated to "bench warmers"? Having faced this issue a number of times in product-centric companies, here are some strategic survival tips from the trenches.

Understand the company's direction by getting the Board and the Executive Team's view on the following questions:

- Is the primary focus revenue growth? Through selling product? Or solutions that include services?
- How important is Customer Satisfaction? Is the company willing to invest to improve this metric?
- Will services become more strategic if it can achieve a positive profit contribution?
- Or is the objective to leverage services to gain market share at any cost? Even if it means a zero or negative services profit contribution?
- How is Sales compensated? Are they motivated to sell Services? Should they be?

The answers to the questions above will help frame the appropriate business model for your team.

For example, in one of my prior assignments, the focus was on revenue growth and significant net contribution to enable the company to obtain a higher multiple from potential investors.

> 🕮 **Thoroughly understanding company direction is important input to the PS business model.**

In this case, we devised a strategy to achieve aggressive revenue targets for services with a net contribution that rivaled the software side of the business. We had a laser-like focus on aggressively hunting for large (multi-million dollar) turnkey fixed-price projects where we could leverage our technology as a key differentiator and deliver the business at a very high gross margin (over 70%). The compensation plans for the sales team were updated to compensate similarly for software and services bookings. This incented Sales to close large turnkey services engagements. Strong delivery processes such as project management, change control, effective use of technology and a just-in-time resourcing model were also keys to our success in achieving high gross margins.

We did end up securing the appropriate multiples for both our software AND services arms!

Ashim Bose, Technology Sales and Services Executive

6 Top Ten Do's for Running a Great Services Organization

In the following list, I provide my view of the areas of greatest leverage for PS management:

- Ensure executive team alignment with your Service strategy. Plan to drive a Services strategy discussion at least annually to ensure alignment.
- Know who your best clients are and why they buy. Create a "top client" program to gain their feedback and commitment.
- Hire the best and the brightest. Promote from within. Reward and celebrate top performers. Constantly recruit top talent.
- Publish goals, objectives and measurements tied to your strategy.
- Create a business model for execution – sales, marketing, delivery, partnering and operations.
- Constantly communicate – continually meet with customers and employees – listen and respond.
- Invest in infrastructure for repeatability – harvest knowledge, IP, tools and techniques. Create a Project Management Office to develop methodology and ensure quality.

- Control your pricing and delivery quality – don't lose money on any deals. Standard pricing, project reviews and contracts are imperative.
- Ensure broad span of control. Drive decision-making close to the client.
- Invest in finance and operations. The only way to drive revenue, profit and utilization is to have complete, accurate and timely visibility to all elements of the business.

Jeanne Urich, Management Consultant, Adexta

7 Focus on Fundamentals

You should never manage with a goal of maximizing profits. Instead you should focus on the fundamentals that drive the business. If you execute on the fundamentals, the profits will take care of themselves.

What are those fundamentals? The top three related to execution are:

Hire the very best people you can find and retain those people. I don't mean hire the best people you can afford or find. I really mean - hire the best people that exist for the job.

If you execute on the fundamentals, the profits will take care of themselves.

Keep those people productively deployed. If they are not generating billable hours, find other value-added activities. Every new company has them. Ask! But, be proactive and find out before you have a bench problem.

Leave a trail of references. Focus on making your customers successful. Finishing a project on time and on budget is just what is expected. Figure out the unexpected. What can your organization do to make your customer truly successful?

And for those who are also responsible for generating demand (otherwise known as selling), there is a fourth fundamental – make sure you have a differentiator for your services. Otherwise, price will be your differentiator.

Aramis Alvarez, VP, World Wide Services, Motive Inc.

8 The Importance of Establishing Your PS Charter

Establishing a clear professional services charter and communicating it effectively to your executive committee and customer base is more critical to success than any other single activity you will undertake in building your PS business.

Your professional services charter will dictate the following aspects of your PS strategy:

- Growth, Revenue and Profit expectations
- The composition of your PS portfolio (Strategy, Technology, Support type offerings)
- Target Markets
- Marketing approach
- PS Delivery structure
- PS Budget

PS leaders who fail to clearly outline and gain agreement on their respective services charter are destined for a future of unrealistic or unmet revenue, portfolio and execution expectations. In fact, it is not uncommon for a perfectly healthy PS business to be viewed as unhealthy because the achieved revenue and profit expectations are being measured against the wrong PS business model.

> **Your PS charter drives everything from portfolio makeup to expectations for revenue and profit.**

Let's look at an example of this. Let's say your PS charter is simply to support the sale of your company's product portfolio. In this case your PS charter could have the following impact:

PS growth may simply be a factor of product growth. Simply put, the expectations for year on year revenue growth should not exceed those of your products. Any expectations that your PS revenue growth might exceed your product revenue growth would be unreasonable.

PS profit targets may not be aggressive. Much of what would normally be considered 'for fee' services (Proof of Concepts, Pre-sales support, strategy assessments) may often be provided 'gratis' as part of a sales opportunity investment. In this case, running a 'break-even' PS business may be an acceptable result.

You may invest little to no Service Marketing dollars as the company markets services as part of their product marketing expenditure. If product-based services are not strategic, but expected, there may be no need to focus on the value of these offerings.

The development of strategic offerings may not be the focus of your portfolio. These services may be provided gratis as part of a pre-sales activity. Implementation and support services, in this case, would be the focal point of your PS offerings. Any investment in developing strategic offerings might be re-directed into developing tools which lower the delivery costs of your product-based services.

Service Delivery management may be incorporated within your sales organizations and aligned geographically, rather than managed separately in an overlay organizational scenario. Since profitability is not as important in this type of PS business as customer coverage and responsiveness, there is less of a need to maximize consultant utilization or to worry about resource sharing across geographic boundaries.

Establishing a well-defined PS charter has the most profound effect on how you structure, report on, invest in and gauge the success of your services business going forward. Effective leadership for your PS business starts and ends with getting continual buy-off of the service business charter and communicating it continually as the business evolves.

Scott Monaghan, Sr. Director, Global Services Engineering, Hitachi Data Systems

9 Why We Exist

After the bubble burst of the early 21st century, our company was starting to dig ourselves out of the mud and muck and I was beginning to build our Professional Services team for the next wave of success. I was putting together a meeting of our growing team (we could all fit in a small hotel room) and wanted to start this team off with a mission... a purpose... something they could carry with them through our clear path to success...or so I hoped. So I decided, as I was sitting on another transcontinental flight, to get out a pad of paper and brainstorm existence statements for our team. For some reason, "more profit, better utilization, more revenue" didn't quite have the impact I was hoping for. So, after a few more hours on a crowded plane, it dawned on me that I was thinking too hard about this. Our job as Professional Services within a software company was actually quite simple. The metrics, measures, percentages, and dollars were not the real goal. They weren't the driving force. What we really did, needed to do, and needed to think about every day was simple, "Create and sustain referenceable customers".

> 🕮 **What we really did, needed to do and needed to think about was simple — create and sustain referenceable customers.**

I tried as hard as I could, but was unable to poke a hole in this one, even though it was so simple. At our meeting I presented this to the team and it received an uninspired series of nods and agreement, but has since been elevated to the rallying cry for everything we do. It has even become an integral part of our recruiting process.

What was amazing and enlightening to me was that this simple, obvious statement has been the driving force for our team for 5 years and continues to be the foundational tenant of our existence. All of the other metrics, measures, percentages and dollars are not to be ignored, but if you get this simple statement right... the other items seem to logically follow.

Toby Cappello, VP Worldwide Professional Services, Lombardi Software

10 When to Make Money

The mistake I have made and have seen made elsewhere is to allow the management team to pressure the professional services organization to deliver profit in the first 12-18 months, when the knowledge gained from the services customer interaction should be more valuable than a small services profit margin. Consulting services should not be "given away," of course, but consulting time needs to be split into billable utilization for the tasks that consultants perform to move the customer from new customer to implemented; and non-billable utilization that keeps the customer engaged in the process of taking on a new software package along with the challenges AND rewards that being an early customer offers. Consultants should be measured and compensated on both types of utilization and not forced to bill when the situation warrants non-bill.

Successfully implemented referenceable customers are the measure of success, not profitability or billable utilization.

In the post-".com" funding environment, the focus for startup software companies has been on achieving profitability early, both as a company and as a professional services organization. A young services organization in a good market implementing version 1.0 product is probably not going to make money initially. A knowledgeable, creative and committed services team has an opportunity that no one else in the company has - to live with those early customers, understand their needs, and communicate those needs effectively back to the organization so that rapid adjustments in product, methodology, sales approach and overall strategy can be made. This early insight ensures the next wave of customers will become profitable in the traditional sense.

Dell recently shifted its support model from a focus on time management, which led to disastrously negative ratings, escalating costs and increasing customer dissatisfaction, to a work-until-resolved approach, which rapidly reversed all those trends (Dell is obviously a much more mature organization, but the lesson holds).

The Professional Service's focus in the early days should be on successfully implemented referenceable customers as the measure of success --- not profitability or billable utilization. Later, as the company matures, the services team can pursue and deliver on all of those objectives.

Robert Freedman, Practice Director, Infor Global Solutions

11 Services Mission and Strategy

Why is your company in the services business? Spending time to understand this from a financial and customer perspective is the most important thing you need to do. Talk with your CEO, your CFO and the sales and marketing leaders. Talk with customers – understand your market segments (high, medium, low or commercial/ government, etc.) and pick a few customers from each segment. Understand the value you are delivering to the company and your customers and summarize it in an overall organizational objectives summary – it doesn't need to be fancy but it does need to "tell your story" and then ensure that all the stakeholders within your company are in agreement and willing to support it. Once you have this ironed out, everything else is a piece of cake! Try to skip this step and you will find yourself stalled and painfully sorting through misunderstandings in the middle of operational activities.

> **Your stakeholders will support you if they understand the value provided by your PSO.**

Beth Martinko, VP Services, Wavelight

12 The PSO's Reason for Being

The Professional Services Organization (PSO) is a key department in the typical technology company these days, but it's often hard to pin down the group's exact mission. After all, products are the main focus, and we've all heard the words "this is a product company, not a services company". So how does the PSO define the right role, one that's clearly aligned with the company's success, and at the same time makes a clear statement of what the group is all about?

We've solved this problem by staking out a three-part mission:

- Achieving customer success – making sure customers are able to get the maximum value from our products and have a great experience doing so.

- Meeting financial goals – operating a successful consulting business with the highest professional standards and sound business results.
- Returning knowledge to the company – sharing useful knowledge gained in the field to improve products, marketing and sales.

The important thing about this mission statement is that the three parts are in order of importance, but all three are necessary. The ability to make customers more successful and satisfied with complex technologies is the main reason companies form PSOs in the first place – without that part the other two are largely pointless. Meeting P&L goals defines the success of the group from the CFO's point of view, and again is necessary for the group's existence. And the practical knowledge that consultants gain in the field has huge value to the company that cannot be captured anywhere else.

A meaningful mission statement defines your charter.

This mission has proved to be durable and useful in a variety of situations in different companies. Mission statements have gotten a bad name, and they deserve it when they are fuzzy, feel-good mishmash. But they are indispensable when they define what your group actually does – and doesn't do.

Matt Kuckuk, VP, Professional Services, Actuate Corporation

13 Managing the PSO in a Product-Centric Company

Successfully leading a Professional Services Organization in a product-centric company is not for the faint of heart. Learn what works.

1. Recognize the Reality

You can't fight city hall...East is east and west is west, and never the twain shall meet...You can call a duck a chicken, but it is still a duck. You have to face the facts: You may well know the huge potential of your organization becoming a high-powered, services-led enterprise, but if you now live in a product-thinking, product-acting, products-are-everything company, it isn't going to happen (at least for a while). So soften your speeches and mind your manners. You are going to have to live with it until the winds of change start to blow in a direction that makes your senior management willing to navigate a new course.

In a product-centric company constantly show how services contributes to the product sale.

2. Demonstrate Your Devotion

You are in a product company, correct? What do product people care about? So show your support by helping sell more products and ensuring that those products are satisfying customers. I'm sure that your services organization is already good at that, but what you may not be good at is continually communicating your contribution to client loyalty, sales growth, and company profitability. Selfishly, this communication is much more important than the actions that spurred it.

Come up with a formula for showing how your great services work helped retain customers and the amount of business your PSO "saved." Don't whine about how your financial results suffered from bailing out the product screw-ups or giveaways; just point out your contribution in time and dollars for the "good of the corporation." This is where the term "good team player" comes in. Deposit the goodwill of your product brethren into your savings account--there will be times when you will need to make withdrawals, but use this sparingly.

3. Sell, Sell, Sell

To make your PSO thrive in a product-centric company, you must sell key customers on your PSO's ability to deliver.

You must sell your team on the vital role they play, and sell them on continuing to excel even when internal circumstances dampen morale. You must sell everyone in the rest of your organization on why your PSO is important, how it contributes to overall success, and why they should change their ways to allow the PSO to make them successful. This is your primary role.

In addition, you must sell your team on selling Sales. To truly succeed, you must have (at least a percentage of) the product sales organization on your side. Your consultants in the field are the vital link.

James A. Alexander, Ed.D., Alexander Consulting

14 Create Strategic Intent

I bootstrapped a PS organization at a small software company about five years ago. Starting with a fledgling group of talented technicians, it was clear that they had no vision for a future state that was broader than simply 'implement our product'. This lack of clarity of purpose denigrated the internal perception of the team to the lowest levels of the organization. In order to attract, retain, and motivate a talented group of consultants it was imperative to create a compelling vision of a future state that extended the mission of the team from simply body-shoppers to being trusted advisors in their respective disciplines. The goal needed to transcend technical value to providing insight into how our customers could achieve better business results. This vision serves to inspire and motivate; it differentiates us as a professional services part of a software company, and allows us to grow our people to add more value as they develop and mature. Regardless of what your particular vision may be, it needs to transcend the operational metrics of the practical business, and serve to show how a person will achieve personal growth.

The talent existing with PS organizations can be used to provide compelling value added services that go way beyond providing just technical services.

Bob Boehnlein, Executive Vice President, Global Services, Aprimo, Inc.

15 Professional Services Top 10

Here's my Top 10 List for a Professional Services Organization:

1. Meet your dates.
2. Build relationships.
3. Manage scope.
4. Estimate – accurately.
5. Don't accept poor implementation quality.
6. Own it! It's not the customer's fault.
7. Manage the customer! (Deer in headlights get run over.)
8. Prospecting: It's everyone's job. Find some gold!
9. Communicate: If you work remotely – don't be disconnected.
10. Maintain intestinal fortitude – courage is required!

Jeff Wilhelm, VP, Global Services – Americas, SupportSoft Inc.

16 Strategic Action

How great would it be if our operations were so well aligned that change would flow smoothly through the organization, and that everyone could work at his or her best? Better have your PS organization ready and the proper scalability mechanisms in place so you don't prevent rapid corporate growth from occurring. Consider these actions as a roadmap to positioning your organization for handling periods of rapid growth:

> 🕮 **Frequently reassess your internal alignment.**

- Instrument a detailed dashboard to detect and monitor trends (acceleration or deceleration of revenue, margin, customer acquisition and retention, by geography, by industry, for each practice).

- Examine your business to reassess the core and the context, and redeploy resources accordingly between proven and new practices.
- Work on career development and employee retention to sustain growth by creating new job responsibilities and service offers.
- Nurture your best and most profitable clients. This is the time to become their trusted advisor. Establish a program office, so you can hear your clients and earn their trust.
- Secure first references, they must be won without ambiguity. Do not forget to negotiate the public use of references up-front.
- Focus on scalability (hiring, training, partnering strategies, acquisition).
- With properly marketed services, selling to early adopters may still be a profitable business and a market segment in which you don't suffer from price pressure.
- Establish practice pioneers by moving the most flexible and highest performing resources from existing practices.
- Work with Product Marketing to design a fully integrated service offering (concept of the "whole product", i.e., the product and all the necessary supporting material and offerings).
- Build a services business plan, based on the product business plan, and highlight to management the necessary investments and impact on margin.
- Get a fresh pair of eyes to look at your projections, a look which will be less emotional, without the bias you may have from the excitement of getting a new product to market.
- Frequently reassess your internal alignment. Our customers love to keep us on our toes, but the excitement shouldn't derail you from your corporate strategy.

Jean Pommier, VP Methodology, ILOG Inc.

2. Organizational Design / Human Resources

This chapter covers topics such as hiring and retention, team building, working with global teams, compensation planning, motivating employees and communication.

"If you hire me to bark at your employees, that will free you for more important things."

17 Winning the War on Talent

We have some great professionals in our recruiting organization but in order to win the "war on talent" and recruit people who are truly the top candidates in their field, we've learned that the recruiting process needs to be a partnership between the recruiting organization and the client-serving areas that need the talent. At the very start of the process the recruiting professionals and the client-serving individuals who will be supporting the recruiting process (by the way, pick your best folks to support your recruiting efforts) need to sit down and determine who will be responsible for which parts of the process. For example, while the recruiting organization may be responsible for conducting initial candidate screenings, tracking candidates through the process, and ensuring supporting documentation gets submitted, individuals from the client-serving organization may need to be responsible for arranging and conducting subsequent rounds of interviews and ensuring that final decisions get made quickly. Once it's been determined up-front who is responsible for what, it goes without saying that the client-serving organization needs to live up to its commitment even though this potentially means having client-serving individuals spending time on a non-billable activity. And, if you're having difficulty getting client-serving colleagues to see the value in dedicating time to recruiting, position it as an investment that supports future business opportunities.

The recruiting process needs to be a partnership between the recruiting organization and the client-serving areas that need the talent.

The importance of taking this type of collaborative cross-functional approach is evidenced by the ill-fated experiment our company tried a few years ago when we outsourced our recruiting function. The outsourcing of our recruiting organization made it much more difficult for the recruiting and client-serving functions to work together and consequently our recruiting performance dropped markedly even though this was at a time when the economy was still soft and the war for talent was less intense. Since we brought the recruiting function back in-house our recruiting performance has improved dramatically. I attribute this to the fact that it is now much easier for those of us in the client-serving organization to work in partnership with recruiting.

Belinda Griffin, Manager, Capgemini

18 Quantifying Recruiting Skills Specifications

Our company was dealing with some leading-edge technologies, and we had to find implementation engineers who could cope well with those new technologies. It was almost impossible to find implementation engineers with prior experience in these areas, but there were related areas in which prior experience was a good indicator for success in assimilating the new technologies. Back in 2004 and 2005 some examples of these new technologies were Macromedia Flex and Enterprise Native XML Databases. Related but more mature technologies were J2EE, Windows SDK and Relational Database. In this tip I refer to the new technologies as X and Y, and the related but more mature technologies as A, B and C.

Quantifying desired skills leads to more effective recruiting.

We came up with a spreadsheet that included descriptions of skills that we needed, an importance rating regarding prior experience in these areas, and the degree of expected use of these skills within our PS organization. Using a value of "10" to signify very important past experience or very high usage within our PS organization, and a value of "1" to signify unimportant past experience or low expected usage, an example spreadsheet looked like:

Skill	Prior Experience	Expected Use Within PS
Skill A	7	3
Skill B	9	3
Skill C	8	8
Skill X	1 or above	8
Skill Y	1 or above	9

This spreadsheet showed we valued past experience in Skills A, B and C, and that we were not spending energy finding people who were experienced in Skills X and Y. The spreadsheet also showed that when working for our PS organization, implementation engineers would use relatively little of Skills A and B, they would continue to heavily use Skill C, and they would be working in an environment that would enable them to develop Skills X and Y.

Through the use of this spreadsheet we were able to easily and clearly convey to recruiters and to applicants the skills desired in our new recruits, how these skills would be used in the jobs within the PS organization, and the new skills that would be developed while working in the PS organization. This method resulted in a much better understanding of our requirements by recruiters and a much-improved flow of candidates who had the most desirable current skills and were enthusiastic about developing specific new skills while working in our PS organization.

Bill Morton, Vice President of Services, Acesis Inc.

19 When the Going Gets Tough, the Tough Have a Meeting

During the downturn of the technology industry in the early 2000s, our organization was re-sized multiple times. A final reduction in workforce consolidated six regions into two - North America and everywhere else. After two months of complete chaos and divided teams, I asked my SVP to allow me to organize a worldwide meeting of the PS resources - all 24 of them. Knowing how incredibly tight our financial situation was, I was not sure he would respond with a resounding "YES". He did say "yes" but - he gave me a budget of $12,000 (not including airfare - thanks for the small favor). In six weeks, the entire team worked together to create agendas, breakout sessions, collateral and input for the meeting. With our budget constraints, the team agreed to share rooms and cars (2 to a room; 4 or 5 to a car); arrive on Thursday night and leave on Sunday (working over the weekend to minimize revenue disruption);

and take the 'lowest-cost airfare option', no matter how painful the itinerary. We spent two and a half days together – eating the continental breakfast included with the room; making sandwiches for lunch from grocery store staples (bread, bologna, cheese, turkey, ham, chips and cookies for an afternoon snack); and adjourning every day by 4:45PM so we could take full advantage of the open bar and light appetizers provided 5 to 7PM at the hotel. It was one of the best teambuilding events any of us had ever participated in. Spending all day and all night planning, working, learning, sharing, supporting, playing, eating and riding together to and from the hotel gave the group a sense of unity that would never have happened otherwise. Never underestimate the value of a face-to-face meeting. It was the best $11, 905.12 we ever spent.

> **Never underestimate the value of a face-to-face meeting.**

Debbie Stovall, VP, Professional Services, SumTotal, Inc.

20 Listen and Engage

You've made it to the executive office... congratulations! You are now at the table and able to drive strategy, and sitting in the board room calling the shots. Don't forget though, that your customers are buying the services of your employees, and it's those very employees who are the face of your company. Make sure you spend at least 20% of your time listening to and talking to the individual contributors who deliver your services.

> **Make sure you spend at least 20% of your time listening to and talking to the individuals who deliver your services.**

If you are new to your role, make sure you let your employees know by your actions, not just words, that you intend to spend time with them and learn from them. If you are in a larger organization, send out a quick survey asking them to tell you what is working, what is not, and solicit their ideas for positive changes. Then call or email everyone who responds to say thank you and follow-up on the information you receive.

If you are in a smaller organization meet with every employee to reinforce that you are on their team and that you are committed to being an agent for positive change on their behalf. You will most likely get a range of responses, from trivial things that bug people to innovative ideas for adjusting your approach to customers. Take care of the trivial things – they may look trivial to you but to service employees who are trying to represent your company to your customers, this stuff gets in the way and diminishes their enthusiasm. Fix them and it's like putting helium in a balloon – it lifts your employees and their ability to serve your customers skyward. Once your employees see you listening and taking action, they will then approach you informally when they have new ideas. And since they see things you will never see in the board room, their insight is invaluable. You do not diminish your leadership by listening to and involving your team. In fact, you create a leadership community where leaders lead at all levels of the organization from the bottom up and back down again. And once established, this leadership community will also accept change much more readily. They understand that you have listened and considered alternatives and that everyone must flow in a single direction. As a result, you'll find yourself spending much less time pushing change in this kind of employee-driven organization.

Beth Martinko, VP Services, Wavelight

21 Maintaining High Standards in Recruiting and Hiring

One of the most important lessons I've learned is not to lower your standards in hiring. Professional services is all about people, and an organization's success and reputation ride on the credibility, professionalism and customer focus of each of its employees. Over the past 15 years, I have learned from good and bad hiring experiences. During this time, I have refined a hiring approach that has helped improve the odds of making a good hire. Five key elements make up this approach:

Five key elements of the hiring process that improve the odds of making a good hire.

Utilize your network to find top talent. I have certainly found top performers through the traditional means of posting to job boards and using recruiters. However, I have had much better success asking employees, industry contacts and others for referrals. Typically, people you know and trust are going to pass along the names of people they know and trust.

Clearly define the type of employee you are looking for. Very often, I am asked to begin a candidate search with, "I just need a consultant" or "We just need good people." Before I go any further in the search, I write a detailed job description for the position, emphasizing the characteristics of the ideal candidate. Technical ability is often cited as the top criteria for a candidate, but, in reality, communication skills, organizational skills, follow-through and professionalism are equally important.

Plan the questions that you will ask during the interview process. My personal experience as a job candidate has proven to me that most people are not very good at conducting an interview. More than anything else, this is the result of poor planning. Before I begin any interview, I document the questions that I will ask based on the characteristics that I've already defined in the job description.

Always check references. References may be the only outside verification that you have of the ability of the job candidate. Reference checks are an opportunity for candidates to market and sell themselves—good candidates view them as such and work hard to provide quality references. I have been surprised at how often a reference was not informed that his or her name was given or the reference didn't have much positive input about the candidate.

Consider third-party testing. I have found the use of personality, psychological and intelligence tests to be another objective measure when assessing job candidates. Two cautions with the use of these tools: (1) make sure you are applying the same testing to all candidates for a job and (2) make sure you fully understand the output of the testing and its relevance to the position prior to using it in your decision-making process

Craig Rozelle, Vice President of Operations, Five9 Technologies

22 Meet Me at the Summit

Never underestimate the need for keeping your consultants happy and motivated. To maintain high levels of employee retention consider organizing a once-a-year tech summit of consultants. This gives the consultants a chance to meet each other, build camaraderie and share knowledge. It also gives consultants a platform to showcase their cool inventions and solutions for others to adopt and follow. Key members of engineering and technical support can also make valuable contributions in this type of forum. The setting needs to be low-key and in a nice hotel away from work - somewhere with plenty of opportunity to socialize and relax.

Javed Maqsood, Director, Professional Services, TriCipher

23 Help Your Consultants Stay Balanced

Advice is easy to give — but sometimes difficult to follow. If I were to advise any consulting executive of one thing, it would be to work to make their consultants well rounded as both consultants and as people. The most successful consultants (and ultimately executives) I have known over my career tend to have qualities that make them "balanced". These individuals not only have the basic technical skills required to do their job, but also have supplemented their skills with strong business acumen and some personal traits that not only make them enjoyable to work with, but also put them in a position to succeed with clients. Successful consultants in many cases turn out to be successful executives, and perhaps even future clients of yours. I have highlighted three areas that I think are the traits necessary to be a "Balanced Consultant".

An investment in developing balanced consultants will have great long-term results.

Technical Skills - Many people perceive the word "technical" to mean strong programming or engineering skills. However, you can actually replace the word technical with any term that shows the individual has a deep understanding of the nuts and bolts of his or her given profession. It could be IT, engineering, research and development, marketing, sales or another area of endeavor. The important thing is to make sure your people work to perfect their "craft." Having a strong area of expertise also means that they continue with the educational process to become better with these technical skills.

Business Skills - There is a chance that you have some individuals who are technically very competent, but lack the business skills necessary to understand and communicate how the work they do makes clients more successful, and ultimately brings in more business. Without these skills it is doubtful that your people will ever grow and advance — something that could impact your career as well. Encouraging your people to develop business skills earlier in their career will put both you and them in a better position to succeed.

Personal Skills - The third set of skills necessary to succeed in consulting work is that of interpersonal skills — in other words how your people interact with others. Even if your people have a deep technical base coupled with strong business skills, they might not interact well with their peers, clients or even you. Working to bring out their non-consulting side will surely go a long way to making them –and you-- more successful. Remember, balance is key.

R. David Hofferberth, P.E., Managing Director,
Service Performance Insight

24 Key Organizational Attributes

For a PS Organization to be successful, there has to be an emphasis placed on the operative word: "Organization".

If a Services Organization is not organized with appropriate skills and clearly communicated responsibilities between groups and teams, the organization can find itself in an environment of chaos and "finger-pointing".

A successful organization should be scalable, and roles and responsibilities need to be discussed and clearly understood. There has to be a common method of communication between groups and between management staff members to ensure teams are working productively and efficiently. PS Executives should look at roles and responsibilities and combine like-roles into one team or one role when possible. This will reduce the number of touch points for success as well as allow you to keep your organization lean and cost effective. Each role should be somewhat specialized, but should also take into account responsibilities of the other team members and actions required to accomplish the organization's goals. This will facilitate appropriate expectation setting with customers and thus provide a solid path to success.

Micheal Eicher, Vice President of Professional Services, Paisley

25 Creating an Environment for Retention

Professional services organizations are continually challenged with identifying, hiring and retaining qualified consultants and engineers who deliver high-quality value-added services for clients. Several factors contribute to the challenge of retaining these individuals which include travel, compensation, and career progression.

Through debriefing sessions over the years with many consultants when they decided to change companies, I have found that the inherent lack of "balance" in their career appears to be the primary motivation. Figure 1 depicts a relatively simplistic view of a balance model that is highly individualistic. There are three main motivational elements for balance in the professional services industry, which include professional, personal and financial balance. Similar to the tire on a car, the distribution of the weight is of paramount importance in ensuring the tire is appropriately balanced for optimal performance. In addition, the application of the weight may differ from tire to tire to attain the maximum performance and balance for that particular tire. Therefore the optimal balance of personal, professional and financial factors is highly individualized for consultants.

The search for "balance" in an employee's career is a primary motivation for changing companies.

Creating an environment that continually enhances career development and growth will support individual balancing requirements.

Consultants have a unique desire to hone their skills, learn new processes, techniques and technologies, as well as provide value-added contributions to their clients. An environment that nurtures and provides these skill-development opportunities will greatly help retain highly valued consulting professionals. The creation of such an environment also assists in creating a sense of community and belonging that is not endemic in the role of consulting professionals.

In order to successfully create a continuous learning environment, it is crucial to identify those individuals who can establish a cornerstone for building such an environment. These individuals are typically identified as being well-balanced, are loyal and truly care about the organization, and have a strong desire to contribute to organizational success. Enlisting these individuals in establishing an ongoing skills- development environment including defining skills-development programs, and identifying appropriate individuals and groups to deliver the skills-development training greatly enhances the probability of success.

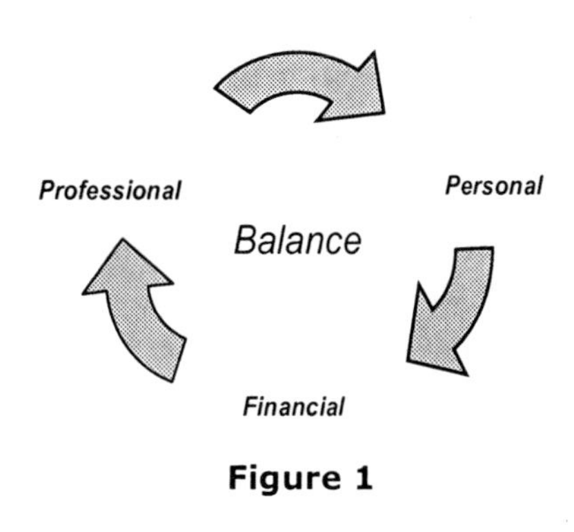

Figure 1

Gerard F. Becker

26 Hiring Right

Hiring the right person, for any job, is difficult. In professional services, the challenges grow as we struggle to find the right balance between technical or functional skills and those intangible skills related to working with clients. I have a litmus test for potential PS hires – they must be passionate about working with external clients.

Hiring right begins with recruiting. It is imperative that the roles and responsibilities for any new hire be clearly defined. Once the job description and the expectations for the position are understood, profiling of the ideal candidate can begin. The profile should include everything you deem necessary in an ideal candidate: personality, background, project experience, technical skills, communication style, seniority, education, great handshake, eye contact, willingness to travel, etc. It is imperative that you be 100% specific about your requirements so that you get the right candidates for consideration.

A litmus test for potential PS hires is that they are passionate about working with external clients.

Once in the interview process, it is critical that you are direct in explaining your expectations to the candidate from the standpoint of the role, ethics, travel, and commitment. In turn, listen carefully to the candidate's expectations and make sure they fit the role, career path, corporate culture, and your own management style. As a practice leader, leave the technical and functional due diligence to your team and instead focus on the personal and organizational fit. If the stars align and you and your team agree that the candidate is a fit, then finish the process with a thorough reference check.

Lest you believe that the hard part is over, it has only just begun. The onus is on you to provide an environment that maximizes the new hire's success. This means clearly defining what is expected of them every day, how they will be trained, how to do expenses and timesheets, how to use the methodology, and how you will manage them. Often overlooked are things like an explanation of the organizational structure outside of their immediate domain as well as company conveniences and good lunch spots. Some companies and managers often think that it is good to test the mettle of new hires by challenging them to figure this stuff out themselves, but I think that approach is counterproductive and expensive. I would rather accelerate a new hire's path to billability.

Finally, ongoing support of your team and your new hires is critical. Don't wait for annual reviews to evaluate and assess your employees. Frequent team meetings, communication, feedback, and personal interaction are important ingredients in the health and well being of your organization. Hire only the best people and remember to trust your intuition. Hire Right!

Carole L. McCluskey, President, EttenAj Consulting LLC

27 The "Armadillo Method" of Team Building Among Remote Consultants

I've found that gathering a team of remote consultants on a regular basis is an excellent way to build a community of disparate team members. One technique to instill a 'bond' among team members is to do something out of the ordinary. One year we gathered our team together in a very remote ranch in western Texas. In addition to some standard training on our software products, we did some fun Texas-style entertainment. Probably the highlight of the event was an armadillo race. Each consultant got an armadillo that they were to coax across a small track. Techniques ranged from verbal encouragement to blowing air near the rear of the armadillo. It was an event that we will never forget. Today, we have an award that we give to the team member who shows the most creativity in their approach. We call it 'The Armadillo'.

Bob Boehnlein, Executive Vice President, Global Services, Aprimo, Inc

28 The Importance of a Well-Written Resume

I've been a recruiter for over ten years in Professional Services and surprisingly, I've seen a lot of bad resumes. Bad resumes equate to lost opportunities. A resume is my first impression of you. If I don't like your resume, I'm probably never going to call you for the interview. On an average search, I probably look at 50-100 resumes. Despite what you might think, I don't read your resume. I scan it very quickly looking for highlights of your career that are relevant to the position and keywords that match up with the search criteria. You could have the greatest skills in the world and be the best fit for the job, but if your resume doesn't articulate your strengths and accomplishments relative to the position you are interviewing for, if it is sloppy, if I find that you've intentionally omitted key information, I will quickly pass judgment on you – not just for this search but for future searches. Recruiters have long memories by the way and a database that tracks every interaction! And please don't stretch the truth! If you were an Associate Partner at Accenture, don't say you were a Partner. If you've managed a team of 5, don't state that you've managed a team of 20. You will likely get tripped up in the interview - without even knowing it. And little white lies can be an applicant's death knell!

Terry Jansen, Founder, PSVillage

29 Working Effectively with Global Services Teams

Every company has a headquarters. Some have more than one to cover the geographic areas of their business. So what happens when you are running a global project with team members focused on their territory? How do you become recognized as a leader if you aren't physically in their office every day? My approach was a bit unorthodox, I'll admit, but it served the global project well in establishing relationships with all territories and respect from the team members.

What was my approach? Give and take geographically. I'm based in the U.S., which is an office within my German-headquartered company. Initial project legwork had to be done with Corporate before anything else. Setting up meetings became my first obstacle - how could I make sure I avoided meeting overruns that would cause me to postpone personal appointments and other global meetings that tend to be in the afternoon? Why not make sure you get all the participants at the start of the day (Central European Time)? That meant 3:00 am meetings weekly (sometimes daily) as I was the only US participant (and luckily on the East Coast!). It was amazing to hear the surprise of people that I would do such a thing. My philosophy was 'they stay late to work with the US, why don't I take the burden this time?'

> **It is amazing what your team will accomplish if you show them there is no center of the world in a global community.**

As the project continued and I worked with other European countries, I adopted the same approach. I was a single person working with one or more individuals in the local offices – doesn't it make more sense to impose on one instead of many? After a while I adopted a Mid-Atlantic time zone internal clock which helped me cover Europe and the Americas easily. When the Asia Pacific Region came on board, I was fortunate that the offices got in early so early evenings meetings were also fine. So what was my benefit? Each country's team members saw what I was willing to do to make them successful and they, in return, did what they could to make me successful. They would stay late for meetings when needed, meet with me on weekends if necessary due to my large amount of travel among the countries, and overall give me their best. I value responsiveness to my team members and their responsiveness back to me. It is truly amazing what your team will accomplish if you show them there is no center of the world in a global community.

Jodi Cicci, Global Project Management Director, Software AG

30 Hiring into Professional Services

To hire the right people into your PS group, make sure that your management team does a good amount of self-reflection and builds consensus around:

- What culture does the management team subscribe to?
- What mix of people do we have in our consulting group? What kind of people will fit in, and who will not?
- What level of independence do we require of our consultants?
- Are we trying to change our direction, purpose and/or focus? Who do we need to help us change these aspects of our group?

Without asking these questions and coming up with some level of consensus for the answers, your hiring managers will be going after candidates that might not have the best chance of succeeding, ultimately affecting your organization as well.

Olga Brown, former Actuate Regional Professional Services Manager

31 Reducing Turnover by Rewarding High Performers

When you look at how expensive turnover is to a consulting organization, you can't help but try a lot of different ideas to reduce turnover. We've been able to achieve a turnover rate (planned & unplanned) of less than 4% by implementing some ideas that at first blush seem like they would be too expensive. I'll discuss a couple of concepts we implemented that, based on feedback, have increased our employee satisfaction.

As part of a software company, the consulting team would always see the sales team going on annual "club" trips in recognition of high performers. We initiated the same reward program for our high performers within the Consulting Services organization. The trip is a 4 day/3 night getaway for those that qualify by hitting pre-defined utilization and quality goals. We encourage the qualifiers to bring their families so we can create very close bonds between our company, the employee and their family. Most members of the team strive for this reward, but also recognize its uniqueness within the operational side of a business.

One of the other challenges the team faced was feeling "connected" in a virtual environment. We started having semi-annual national meetings. These events bring the entire consulting team together for company updates and team specific break-out sessions. More importantly, the team members get a chance to reconnect with each other and establish new relationships with new team members. We typically schedule these meetings at the end of a week or beginning of a week, so the employees can bring their families. Not only are the families welcome at the events and meals, but it gives us another chance to make a tighter connection with our employees.

Since putting both of these ideas into action, the feedback from the team has been very positive. We have also seen our turnover rate remain very low, even during highly competitive job market cycles.

When both of these ideas were originally floated, most of the feedback was that it would reduce margins and take the team out of the field for too long, costing us lost revenue. Quite the opposite has occurred. I'm confident that the investment made in these meetings and the annual reward trip is easily offset by the cost that would be associated with key employees resigning.

Jon Harris, Chief Service Officer, Ultimate Software

32 Minimizing the Challenges Inherent in a Geographically Dispersed Group

I ran a 50 person team for Siebel Global Services for several years. About two-thirds of the team was in the US and one-third in EMEA and APAC. Most of my consultants were traveling every week and often into other geographic regions within the US or between the US and APAC or EMEA. It was important to me that my people didn't 'go native'. 'Go native' is a phenomenon where a consultant identifies more with the customer or other groups within your company than they do with their own team. This is particularly challenging with a geographically dispersed group although it can happen with local consultants too.

It was important that my people didn't "go native" --- identifying more with the customer than with their own teams.

Regular communication is key. I had a geographic lead in EMEA and APAC. My US team was organized along skill specialty. We had weekly calls for all consultants. All consultants currently working in EMEA were on the EMEA call with the EMEA geographic lead, myself and my US-based specialty leads. Same for APAC. Each of my US Leads had a call with their US based sub-team. That way, everyone in the practice got 'touched' at least once a week and was kept informed about what was going on in the company, in the practice and in their sub-team.

Whenever possible, everyone in the practice either saw me or one of the leads in-person at least once a quarter. I also had a virtual open-door policy. People in my team knew that they could come to me with anything and that we all were part of a team. Siebel regularly surveyed employee satisfaction and we consistently had the highest ratings, low attrition and lots of people wanting to transfer in.

Michael Resnick

33 Create a "No Surprises Culture"

Even in an environment where we hire the "best and the brightest" consultants, we often find ourselves left in the dark until the last minute about unhappy clients. The problem: many of the best consultants are not good at delivering timely bad news and will do whatever they can to fix a problem rather than alerting you to it in time for you to make a difference. The result is that too often as a leader in a services organization you don't get the opportunity to fix client relationships before they go sour.

The best way to prevent this problem is to create what I call a "No Surprises Culture". Make sure your consultants know that you do not like to be surprised by a call from an irate customer, and that it is always OK (even a good thing!) to deliver potentially bad news. There are many ways to build this culture in your organization. For example, always lead by example, and never over-react to a situation when first confronted with a problem. If your consultants know they can come to you with a problem and still leave with all their limbs attached, they will! Make this culture even more pervasive by building the concept into your systems and your business processes. Establish meetings, reports, and other situations that will promote discussion about engagement issues. Take advantage of services management systems that have real time dashboards that can be configured to give you a complete view of all of your client engagements (good and bad!). In short, make sure your organization is set up to make sure you are never surprised by that angry customer call.

Make sure your consultants know that they can always come to you to deliver potentially bad news.

Justin Foster, NetSuite Inc.

34 Never Underestimate the Power of Incentives

I was managing a good sized PS group (50) in a fairly young company ($25M) and the emphasis was on revenue, revenue, revenue. We established a bonus plan for the PS group that was almost exclusively focused on PS revenue and even compensated Sales for services business. Well, we took the hill—blew through our targets and all got great bonuses. It turns out that services revenue was easier to get than product revenue and, unfortunately, those were the days when too much service revenue was looked upon unkindly. Our investors got very, very worried that they were in a services business. Needless to say, the following year we had a more "balanced" bonus plan.

> 🕮 **Structure your bonus plan very carefully.**

The lesson learned: never underestimate the motivational power of incentives, or the ability for a motivated team to reach the goals set out for them – especially if lots of compensation is involved. Make sure you know what you are asking for and structure the incentive plan very carefully to get it.

Alvin Begun, Begun Consulting

"Nobody came back from the Goal Setting Workshop. They all left to find better jobs."

35 Developing an Effective Interview Process

Building effective teams begins with the hiring process. Here the focus needs to be to ensure that recruits are effective team members rather than standout individuals.

Any group serious about building a truly effective team must start from this point of view, and involve a cross section of the team in the interview process. This involves a significant amount of trust on the part of the hiring manager who truly must "walk the talk".

Key points in the interview process are:

- Have the candidate interview with 3-4 members of the team. Only one of these interviews needs to focus on the "technical" requirements of the position. The other interviews are more concerned with the cultural and values aspects – i.e., how will the potential recruit fit in to the corporate culture, and the team environment.
  Note: The cultural interviews need take no more than 30 minutes, and can be carried out synchronously – i.e., there is no need for the candidate to come back multiple times.

> 🕮 **Ensure that recruits are effective team members rather than standout individuals.**

- Ensure you have a representative interview panel. This should ideally be comprised of:

  - Human Resources person

  - Line Manager

  - Someone competent to assess technical skills (may be the line manager, depending on the role)

  - A Team Member who would be a peer of the successful candidate

- Have all interviewers complete a standard assessment sheet to ensure that they are adopting a consistent evaluation. At a minimum, this should include sections on the following:

  - Cultural fit
  - Work experience
  - Communication skills
  - Potential
  - Leadership/Managerial skills

Each section should have a numeric rating e.g., 1-5, and a section to write free-form comments.

Once all interviews have been completed, the interview panel should convene as a group as soon as possible to review their individual assessments and rank the candidates.

All members of the panel have an equal voice, and if any member of the panel votes against a candidate, that candidate is excluded from further consideration. This can be the most difficult part for a line manager, but it is extremely important for team members to feel part of the process, and to give of their time.

Kevin Hanvey, Executive Director, Taking Aim Pty. Ltd.

36 "Blending" Technical Field People Across Multiple Roles

Early stage startups like to run as lean as possible. One of the ways they can do that is by "blending" technical field people across multiple roles. The logic follows that "hey, if you're technical and presentable, then you should be a good consultant or an SE, right?" While that may be a great way to start, you run the risk of growing a team with good generalists, but without any great Sales Engineers or great Consultants... and great companies need great specialists.

In an early stage startup with 2-3 sales reps, while the first customers are getting deployed and referenceable, having chameleons in the field provides a number of benefits. You get consistency between the team that sells and the team that implements. This means one fewer surprise for your early customers, and if you're an early-stage start up, your first customers are probably already getting more surprises than they need. Because your first deployments will likely be pilots and generally part of a larger sales process, you will need both sales and services skills to make those first deployments successful.

Once you start transitioning beyond the first couple of deployments, and the customer base and sales team start growing, you will need to start hiring distinctly different people. SEs and Consultants are two very distinct skillsets and generally two very different personality types. I've managed both SEs and Consultants in the past, and I would best characterize SEs as "sprinters" and Consultants as "distance runners".

When do you transition from a blended team of chameleons to dedicated SEs and Consultants?

So the big question is when do you transition from a blended team of chameleons to dedicated SEs and Consultants? I suggest transitioning as early as possible. If you've been managing them as one group, be ready and willing to transition the SEs into the Sales organization if and when that is the right thing to do. Don't try to manage both groups beyond the point when it makes sense. They should eventually be on different comp plans and SEs should start building a close alliance as soon as possible with their sales reps. As early as possible, the Services organization needs to start treating SEs as "beta customers" for your training programs. If you can't effectively train internal people that you don't manage, good luck training customers. Most importantly, though, start hiring specialized people as soon as you can. "Chameleons" are very important to an early stage organization, but you will want to get "A" players in your SE organization and "A" players in your consulting organization as soon as possible.

Nello Franco, VP, Services, W5 Networks

37 Right People, Right Seats, Right Bus

Everyone knows that one of the most difficult tasks in a people-centric business such as managing a Professional Services organization is hiring and retaining good employees. I learned a useful tool from a management training class I took a few years ago that has stood the test of time.

That tool or concept is as follows: "Get the right people on the bus and in the right seats, and get the wrong people off the bus". This initially may sound a little harsh but it does prove itself out in the long run. In fact, I have a little yellow bus from that class that sits on my desk and I use as a reminder every day. When I think back to difficult personnel situations in the past and how they could have been handled differently (or better) I think of this little prop and, had it been applied in those instances, could have saved me and my management team many hours of headaches.

> 🕮 **Get the right people on the bus and in the right seats --- and get the wrong people off the bus.**

There are many analogies which can be made but if you have the "wrong" people on the bus, (i.e., people that do not have a consultative personality or bad attitudes) chances are no amount of training or coaching experience is going to resolve that situation. It's better to get them off the bus.

Alternatively, if you can find good people and get them "on the bus" you may not have them in the right seat initially, but chances are you will eventually find the right seat for them and they will be good performers. It is also important to recognize that the consulting business is a long journey. People may encounter bumps in the road either in their personal lives or simply want to grow in a different direction career-wise in order to have new challenges. That's OK and you simply look for a different seat on the bus for them.

This may seem like an overly simple concept but if applied consistently in the management of a Professional Services organization it will work.

Kevin Fawver, IBM

38 Removing the "Dis" from a Consulting "Disincentive" Plan

Discussing consulting incentive plans in my organization often results in a very lively, tense, impassioned and usually unproductive meeting. This wasn't always the case; there was a time when everyone involved was at peace with our incentive plan structure. In fact, it used to run so smoothly I couldn't imagine how my job could possibly get any better. Then a few years ago, the earth's core seemed to shift and the stability of the Consulting Unit abruptly changed when the company's executives revised the structure of the consultants' incentive plan. The former plan paid quarterly incentives to individual consultants based on each consultant's utilization rate versus a pre-defined goal. The plan details were straight forward, and the highly motivated consultants typically made out very well while less motivated or junior consultants were encouraged to perform better.

> 🕮 **Some day, when the memory has faded and the wounds have healed, we will embark on another incentive plan strategy.**

During a period of reduced consulting sales, the Consulting Unit's margins were suffering while we paid bonuses to some individuals while others sat idle on the bench, did non-billable work for clients or worked on in-house projects. As it turned out, some (now former) consultants were quite comfortable resting on the bench. Bottom line, the unit did not generate enough margin dollars to fund the incentive bonuses. To fix this problem, we launched a new incentive plan that was based on group goals as well as individual ones. Individuals still had goals to meet under this new plan, but they only received a bonus if the group as a whole met its revenue goal and, some felt, if the moon was full. Basically, every individual in the group had to meet or exceed his or her utilization goal before any payouts were made. The new plan made sense from a financial perspective, because it protected the profit center's margin. But the new plan was a "disincentive" plan to individuals because the group goal was not being met. Unit morale quickly crashed and the unit members started to resent each other.

We resolved the problem by eliminating the incentive plan altogether and boosting individual base salaries to be commensurate with contribution and performance. Someday, when the memory has faded and the wounds have healed, we will embark on another incentive plan strategy.

Daniel Peyron, VP of Professional Services, Shaker Computer & Management Services, Inc.

39 Learn to Love Odd People

"Entrepreneurial Life" is a book authored by Bo Peabody. Bo was the founder of a company when he was 19 called Tripod and which he went on to sell to Lycos for about $60M before his 28th birthday. He makes a couple of key points about entrepreneurial success that I saw first hand at Clarify.

Bo points out that in order to even have a chance in starting a successful company you need to have an idea that is fundamentally innovative, morally compelling and philosophically positive. I believe we had that at Clarify and also in our PSO. I think that we truly had some fantastic technology and that we really wanted to see our customers create a fundamentally different and better experience for their customers. We also passionately wanted to see our PSO employees be successful.

> 🕮 **It's the odd, weird and brilliant people who will make you successful as a PS leader.**

This brings me to another one of Bo's suggestions and my tip for this book. "Learn to Love the Odd People".

First of all, you need to have this fundamentally-innovative, morally-compelling and philosophically-positive idea to attract these odd people. If you have this like we had at Clarify you're in luck, because it's these odd, weird and brilliant people that will make you successful as a manager and leader in professional services. The good news is that you don't have to be odd yourself to attract these folks. In fact, the more ordinary you are the better. There is some kind of great symbiotic relationship between the "normal" manager or leader and the "less normal" but brilliant consultant. You just need to truly care about them - you can't fake it. They are the "A" students and they'll see through you very quickly. Once you have them on your side, they will be the hardest working, most intelligent and inspired members on your team.

I definitely experienced this first-hand when I managed the Alliances and Certification team. Coming from Marketing, my team did not look like, talk like, smell like or even care about the things that the people I worked with in Marketing at HP, DEC or Clarify ever did. However, my consultants were incredibly passionate about our products, dedicated to our goals and I could count on them to work some pretty tremendous hours to get the job done. All a relatively ordinary "B" student like me needed to do was to listen carefully to their concerns, let them come up with the solutions and give them the creative space and support to get the job done.

So my tidbit – learn to love your weird and different consultants if you want to be successful.

Bob Bates, Former Director, Clarify and Founder, Resolve Today LLC

40 Know Where the Money Comes From

In the market place, Merger & Acquisitions should create savings from synergies in the back office support organizations. In other words, you don't need two accounting groups. In an aggressive attempt to realize savings as we went through our own M&A, we decided to release all but two accounting resources from the acquired group. With 10 people out the door, out went the information about how to determine billed amounts on projects to date, how much money customers stilled owed us for fixed fee project work and what to do when no one else knows what to do with the 1001 spreadsheets containing various parts of the data needed for the above. We spent months figuring it out. So before any reduction in workforce, know: who owes you what; when it is due; and how you are going to get it. ALWAYS know where the money comes from.

Debbie Stovall, VP, Professional Services, SumTotal Systems, Inc.

41 Quickest Path to Growing a Services Revenue Stream

If you are on the hook to quickly grow a services revenue stream, the first item you should look at is compensation. Assuming your team is in place, nothing separates the hunters from the farmers quicker than a commission-based compensation plan. Aggressive sales professionals, whether they are on the license side or services side, prefer commission-based compensation programs with accelerators for over-achievement. This is how they maximize their incomes. My experience shows that when a program of this nature is put in place, the organization turns around rapidly. The change management issues associated with this type of change are significant, so spend a good deal of time developing the plan (and gaining plenty of input), communicating it to your leadership team, and rolling out the plan to your sales team. Expect lots of exceptions the first year, and prepare your finance or sales support teams for the increased burden. Your delivery teams will need to be prepared for the growth, and their hiring and training plans need to be underway. The bookings and backlog will increase, but ultimately, the company will be counting on your team to deliver with high-quality results.

🕮 **Aggressive sales professionals prefer commission-based compensation programs.**

Keith Costello, SVP Consulting, SAP

42 Six Tenets of PSO Leadership

1. The Rule of Three - The vast majority of people (even really smart people) can hold only three goals, or three issues, or three ideas in their mind at one time. That seems to be the maximum. So when you have a rule that holds up, don't violate it. Limit your organization's primary goals, critical issues, and top tasks to three--no

🕮 **Six rules to become a great Services Leader.**

more. If you can live by this rule, you will see that life becomes much easier. The Rule of Three is also a maxim of good communication--limit your message to three main points and your power of persuasion will go up dramatically.

2. Separate the Vital Few from the Useful Many* - Now you may say, Rule 1 sounds good, but I still have to deal with these 26 KPI's I got from the big boss. We understand that this is reality. However, you do have the power to focus on the few—to concentrate your best efforts on the top three that will have the most impact. Rank your goals and tasks, concentrate on the top three, and determine the absolute minimum effort required to meet the bare minimums of the rest. Delegate as many as you can (in the name of developing your people!), and try just forgetting the least important and see what happens. More often than not, no one cares.

*This phrase comes from Joseph Juran, one of the giants of the quality movement.

3. Before You Giveth, First Taketh Away - Next, think about your people and your role in helping them be more successful. Before adding one more dipper to their overflowing bucket of work, first think through what can be dumped out to make room. Ask them (no, require them) to rank their tasks in consideration of accomplishing their responsibilities, and eliminate any "nice to do" items. They will respect your wisdom, appreciate your consideration, and contribute more to the things that truly matter.

4. Focus on the Crop, Not the Plow - A natural state of affairs (particularly for those of us who are engineers) is to get caught up in methods and procedures of "how things are done." This is all well and good when specific projects are necessary to mend procedures, streamline processes, or fix a bad model. You'll get better results with less effort, however, if you quit micromanaging the tilling and the planting, and just monitor the desired harvest yield. Besides, if you have the right people on your crew, they can do the work better than you anyway. Give your people clear, aggressive goals and the tools to accomplish them. Then get out of the way.

5. Unbridle Your Horses - Every organization (hopefully) has a few stars that you depend on. Let us guess--you reward these top players by assigning them the toughest problems you have. Correct? You are missing a huge opportunity! To make the biggest gains (and, thus, make your life easier), challenge your mid-level performers to demonstrate their capability by giving them the organization's problems to fix. Reward your horses by letting them take on the big opportunities that may lead to significant revenue opportunities or create competitive barriers. By doing so, you will unleash their true potential by letting them demonstrate their leadership.

6. Just Say No - The natural tendency of anyone brought up in the services industry is to say yes. Yes to helping a client out with something "just a little" beyond scope. Yes to meeting marketing's seemingly endless requests for showcase account examples. And yes to bailing out a salesperson that promised a ridiculous date on a client go-live. In fact, yes is often the first word that comes out of a service professional's, services manager's, or services leader's mouth.

In many situations, this is the right thing to do--suck it up for the good of the client, your colleagues, and the company. A little extra effort on your part can do a lot of good. It is worth it.

Yet, there are some very negative aspects of saying yes too often. Based upon your agreeable past behavior, you set an unrealistic expectation with the people that you deal with, as they assume you will always say yes to any requests. So when the customer or the salesperson or the marketer comes to you with a truly outrageous request and you refuse, he looks at you with disbelief and mutters phrases such as "I wonder what has gotten in to him! Or, "she must be having a really bad day."

Furthermore (and, of course, it was not your intent), you establish a perception that you are a pushover. So your attempts at being a good team player backfire, and you are seen as being a weak manager.

So what is the answer? If you have fallen into the "pattern of yes" described above, you can't just start saying no anytime you feel justified, or you'll get the reaction described earlier--it is too abrupt a change. You have to earn the right to say no. You accomplish this by making a "just say no" personal strategy. Do your homework up-front by defining appropriate boundaries of what you will do and what you will not do while supporting the overall business. Involve senior management in the process to gain agreement on how to handle the special requests that you know from experience will occur, and get their commitment on how they will be handled. By involving other executives, and by having fair plans on what is acceptable and what is not, not only can you "do the right thing" for the business, you can build and maintain your own personal credibility.

Say yes when it counts, but just say no when it doesn't.

James A. Alexander, Ed.D., Alexander Consulting

43 Separate Performance and Career Development Reviews

Quarterly, semi-annual, or annual performance reviews should focus on what the consultant did and achieved over the review period. This review is the foundation of the performance bonus or if needed, disciplinary action. Career or Capability Development reviews should focus on the progression of the consultant's capabilities over the review period. This review is the foundation for promotions, new project roles and learning actions. It's possible for someone to have achieved a lot during the review period but to not have progressed in capability development. This person would deserve a big performance bonus but should not be promoted.

> **Separate the actual feedback sessions for performance and career development reviews.**

While there are some synergies in combining data gathering for both reviews, separate the actual feedback sessions, if possible. First meet the consultant to talk about what he/she did well and areas for improvement during the performance period and determine the performance bonus and/or disciplinary actions. Then, conduct a separate capability review session (if it was not possible to schedule the sessions separately, I would physically walk out and then come back in the room). Use this session to explicitly talk about the movement the consultant made in various capability categories, and then discuss promotion issues and specific improvement/learning actions.

George Chen, Principal, Strategos

44 A Unique Training Approach

We all know how important it is to train our people on our technology and on critical business practices such as project management and quality management. It is almost impossible to get a competitive advantage in these areas. However, there is one area of training that few leaders are aware exists and even fewer have properly leveraged -- teaching people how the mind works and how to use that knowledge for business purposes. No, this is not about exhorting people to think positively. The probability of that succeeding is about equal to the success rate of New Year resolutions.

> 🕮 **This training technique gave my people an almost miraculous ability to manage change, and to set and achieve "impossible" goals.**

Over my 30+ years in the business, I have seen an uncounted number of "critical initiatives" of one sort or another come and go. Most never achieve the original objectives or sustain that achievement very long. However, I learned about, and used a technique in Digital Equipment Corporation during the '80s that I then applied in Oracle during the '90s, and most recently in Openwave. This technique is based on formal research in the field of cognitive psychology. It gave my people an almost miraculous ability to manage change, set and achieve "impossible" goals, think in ways that fostered successful innovation and made it extremely easy for me and my management team to lead effectively. This has helped me launch new business initiatives, change operational methods, deal with downsizing while demand was ramping up, and a host of other challenges.

What is this training? The training teaches how the points of view we hold about ourselves, others in the company, customers, competitors, market conditions, and so on, set limits on what we believe is possible, or even permitted, for us to achieve. These beliefs are very often incorrect, but they are self-reinforcing. The training helps people to understand what is going on, how it is holding them back, and how to use that knowledge effectively. A side benefit of the training is the dramatic improvement in the person's overall quality of life. The effect on employee morale and motivation has always been substantial. (Once a person knows how to achieve higher goals in the work environment, they know how to achieve any goal in any part of their life.)

What should you look for in a provider of this training? Track record and references. This training has been going on without fanfare for decades so your training provider should be able to show a long list of reference clients from business, government, non-profit organizations, professional sports teams, and so on. Check the references. There is a lot of junk science in the market and many people are exploiting it. Don't get caught up in their claims.

Implement this type of training with your team and see what happens. I was amazed when I did it. I am confident you will be amazed at the outcome too.

James G. Neumann, VP/GM Global Services, Causative, Inc.

3. Business Operations

This chapter covers topics such as utilization, revenue and margin management, capacity planning, pricing strategies and project estimating.

"My sources tell me you're not happy with your job. So we've decided to forget all about productivity and profits and start making your happiness our #1 priority."

45 Use a Site Survey to Resolve Scheduling Constraints

When our sales were ramping faster than we could staff up our services, we were challenged to start the new projects within 30 days of contract signing. Our backlog was approximating 90 days, so the only way to start projects sooner was to pull people off existing projects at the risk of alienating those customers. In the face of this challenge, we made a profound observation: although the new customers were eager to have their projects started, their IT departments were never really ready to commit their own resources. In effect, they had tighter resource constraints than we did. So we created the Site Survey. This was completed the first billable week in each project. We hired a mature individual who could develop a good rapport with customers. (He had a teaching background with experience in IT.) We armed him with a site survey document, which was a lengthy planning document that the customer would need to work through. Our Site Survey Manager would visit new customers shortly after the contract signing and spend as much time as they needed working through all of their preparedness issues: location of servers, dedicated network equipment, third party software, scheduling stakeholders from other departments, etc. Customers would invariably ask us to give them several more weeks of preparation time. This approach worked wonders: new customers had the 'pride of ownership' to see their project get started; existing customers would complete their implementations uninterrupted; and best of all – we avoided the problem of idle time - having billable resources standing idle at customer sites. With a 90-day backlog, life was good!

We avoided the problem of idle time – having billable resources standing idle at customer sites.

Joe Longo, VP Professional Services, MetricStream

46 Better Project Estimating

When doing project estimation, have you often wondered how to incorporate your project execution experience, methodology, and the various steps involved in implementing a product into more of a science rather than the art of using the quintessential spreadsheet? I have worked for many companies who did project estimation in an Excel spreadsheet, which was not only inefficient but was based on the experience of the person doing the estimating. Not surprisingly, it was never accurate, many things were overlooked, and there often was no ground to stand on behind the numbers. All that changed when I joined a company and was exposed to a technique to use MS Project to achieve a perfect services estimates package that can be delivered as part of the pre-sales cycle. First, we used MS Project to mimic our entire methodology and detailed execution steps under each phase of our methodology. Each of the tasks in MS Project was fully loaded with resources and rate sheets, and was fully predecessor-based. All assumptions were documented at the bottom of the project plan which included variables/parameters which would change effort estimates. To complement the entire process, we created a scope matrix document that our sales/ pre-sales/PSO folks could complete while engaged in various conversations that took place during the pre-sales cycle. This process enabled them to provide prospects with an estimate on the spot. Within the scope matrix document, all we had to do was complete the assumptions, enter the parameters and change any effort estimates (we usually used the color blue for variable-based tasks) in the project plan. Once we did that, we used the MS Project plan document to generate: a) a high level project Gantt chart b) an assumptions document (very important) c) a resource mix required for the project (customer and vendor) and d) a quote document. All these documents, which were absolutely critical in the pre-sales cycle would be generated out of the project-plan document. What were the advantages? Well, when you put a 500-step project plan in front of a prospect with well-documented

> 🕮 **Good project estimating boosts credibility and helps reduce negotiation cycles.**

assumptions, it becomes very obvious that you've done your home work. It boosted our credibility and helped reduce negotiation cycles with the customer. This was hugely successful for our PSO as finally there was some science behind our project estimation process.

Mahesh Baxi, Sr. Director, Professional Services

47 Setting Realistic Utilization Targets

When deciding on a billable utilization target for your consulting team make sure to factor in time for training, travel, vacations, holidays, etc. Targets between 75% and 85% are reasonable for most professional services organizations although they may vary for different individuals and teams or at different points in the company's development. Realistic targets help to prevent burnout, turnover and ensure consultants can effectively meet their customers' needs. You may also want to consider tracking investment utilization as well to ensure that learning, methodology and other knowledge development initiatives are being "funded" by the efforts of people on the team. For a smaller company without a well-developed knowledge base or methodology, these investments can pay off over time in greater use of templates and repeatable best practices.

Realistic utilization targets help to prevent personnel burnout and turnover.

Patrice Reid, Project Director, Comergent

48 Fixed-Fee Arrangements

While the standard position is to always do time-and-materials arrangements for services related to software, fixed-fee arrangements may be very useful in the early days of a software company:

- Recognized revenues and margin are typically not yet critical; bookings are more important.

Fixed-fee arrangements show the customer that you have faith in and commitment to your company's products.

- You will probably need to overstaff anyway to ensure solid customer references and overcome any early domain experience skill shortages.
- Fixed-fee arrangements show the customer that you have faith and commitment to the product.
- Make sure that the arrangement defines an end state for the project which will enable you to extract key resources for other projects.

Thomas Murphy, VP Professional Services, Integrien Corporation

49 Evaluating Project P&L

Evaluating project profitability is one of the most important jobs we have. Attaining margin targets in a growing organization is a huge challenge. Not meeting your margin target could be symptomatic of many other problem areas in the business. Or it could be that you were never able to get profitable with the discounting that was offered in the sales process. In order to help understand the actions that need to be taken to improve margin, we created P&L reporting that included an estimate of the discount percentage on the deal. We also added a slippage factor (defined as the original estimate minus estimate to complete divided by the estimate to complete). This enabled us to quickly see on a customer basis where the biggest issue was --- in the execution of the project or in the original discount offered.

Including discount data in P&L reporting leads to a better understanding of PSO performance.

Gail Scearbo, Consultant, PS Executive

50 Look for a Simple Solution First

I was involved in a systems implementation for a very large, worldwide express company. The company had decided it was time to update their technology in an effort to streamline the time from package pickup to delivery. They pulled out all the stops and were examining all of their technology in use at the time. In this case though, the company had one service location that was plagued with the logistical challenge of having their container truck reach planeside in time for the evening departure of the cargo flight to the central hub. To resolve this issue, they enlisted the help of all the systems experts on staff and they also engaged their software vendors to review all the shipping software to identify ways to extend their products to save time at the loading dock. They involved their own industrial engineers and efficiency experts, armed with their calculators and stop watches, to measure the nano-seconds required to perform activities such as picking up a package, setting it on a conveyor and rolling it into a cargo container. This was looking like it would be an extremely expensive endeavor, and we were not looking forward to presenting the cash outlay required to re-engineer their business processes and logistics systems to shave the 15-30 minutes the truck was so routinely delayed by.

📖 **Solutions do not need to be complicated to achieve great results.**

To resolve this, we suggested they put a second person in the passenger seat of their truck and use the commuter lanes to reclaim the needed time.

Elaborate and expensive solutions are not always the best. Don't get too caught up looking for technology to solve business issues.

Anonymous

51 Utilization 101

When I first started managing business operations for professional services, I dutifully reported on key metrics including utilization, revenue per headcount, cost, and project profitability. Over time, I learned that managing utilization is the FIRST STEP toward increasing revenues and profitability.

The revenue formula is very simple:

revenue = rev/day * headcount * (billable utilization % * 260 workdays/year)

There are only three levers that we can affect. We can change the price per hour and leverage value pricing (typically fixed-price bids) to increase the average revenue per day. We can change the headcount. And, we can set and manage billable utilization rates. I use the word "manage" because we cannot arbitrarily, or significantly, increase these rates over time.

Comparing actuals to target billable utilization rates supports key organizational decisions:

> 🕮 **Managing utilization is the first step toward increasing PS revenues and profitability.**

- HIRE if we are at or exceeding the targets and the backlog is strong
- INCREASE pre-sales support if we are below the targets and the backlog is weak
- CHANGE the skill mix if we are below the targets and the backlog is growing (i.e., the skill mix does not support the business)

Utilization is a primary metric for professional services. It really does reveal a lot about the health of the organization.

Glenda Aune

52 Practice Firmness with Flexibility

Being a good Project Manager means walking the line of being flexible and accommodating to a customer, yet being firm and driving issues to resolution when the customer Project Manager is unable or unwilling to do so. A Project Manager should always at least give the customer team an opportunity to "do the right thing" before escalating an issue that could be damaging to the team member within the customer organization. However, acknowledge that sometime this is what you will have to do in order to make the project successful.

Anonymous

53 Advantages of a Fixed-Price Contract

Like many of you, I grew up with the mentality that Time and Material engagements were ALWAYS better. In theory that is true, but I have found that, in reality, they seldom are. If you are willing to walk away from the customer engagement, then Time and Material is the way to go, but how many times does that happen? Especially if you are running services for a software company that values follow-on business or a reference customer.

> 🕮 **T&M engagements aren't necessarily better than fixed price engagements.**

The only difference between a T&M and a fixed-price project is who suffers or benefits from the accuracy of your estimate. That's it. What about scope changes you say? Any well-managed project, T&M or Fixed, should address this. Every estimate is based on assumptions and a scope. If either one changes, you are then able to change your estimate. Done well, you should be able to get your change request regardless of the model.

Time and material becomes a lose/lose proposition. Under this model, if you come in under your estimate, you pass on the savings to the customer. But if you go over your estimate, are you able to continue charging? Most of the time, I cannot. Legally I can, but politically I cannot. Forcing the issue will, in most cases, make that engagement the last engagement with that customer. How many times have we heard the comment, "I would not have purchased your software if you had not misled me on the cost of implementation......"?

With fixed pricing, if we deliver for less than the bid, our company benefits from coming in under budget thereby increasing our profit. And if we exceed our estimate, we will eat it just the same as with T&M. In addition, we avoid many of the sales arguments associated with billing rates or the resources assigned to the project – like offshore.

Aramis Alvarez, VP, World Wide Services, Motive Inc.

54 Managing P&L Statements

After managing P&Ls for consulting business units at two Fast 500 companies, I suggest the following guidelines:

Blame it all on Sales - That usually doesn't work so you better keep reading!

Top Line Priority - The CFO just provided a massive budget spreadsheet with all sorts of line-item details and formulas. From your analytical nature and likely technical background you believe that crunching the numbers and focusing on the spreadsheet on an ongoing basis will make this fiscal year a success. STOP! You can't save your way into substantial P&L success. You have to sell your way into P&L success! Imagine your P&L responsibility as a lake. You can do the back-breaking work of trying to remove the large, sharp rocks, and even after they are removed, the lake is dry and not navigable. Better to work on covering the rocks with water to ensure smooth sailing. A prudent review of costs and ongoing expense management is required, but focus more on maximizing revenue.

> 🕮 **Time urgency and customer retention sometimes trump price and margin.**

Urgency beats Price - You can't go back in time and make bench hours billable. In terms of P&L management, far better to sacrifice an hourly margin or compromise on a list rate to gain revenue rather than absorb pure bench time. Even with fixed-price deals, it can make sense to offer a discount to get the project started earlier if you are faced with bench time. I'm not advocating undue risk on lightly scoped fixed price deals, but I am advocating discounts to start a well planned effort sooner.

Align Metrics - Our average utilization is strong, consultants are crowing about their utilization performance but we're missing the bottom line target on my P&L. How can that be? Utilization rates are likely being used as an assumption in the P&L model, but the real business measure is revenue not the number of hours. Seek to measure consultants on revenue to ensure they are aligned with the standard financial measurements of business (and your bonus metrics).

Keep the Customer – As much as you want to hit your numbers, it's better to sacrifice some margin to keep a good customer happy. Your bonus may suffer and your boss may be somewhat unhappy, but the business will be better off keeping the customer relationship and reference. That being said, remember that a "good customer" is one who pays their bill in a timely manner and has at least the potential to buy more services.

Matt Jacobson, Vice President Professional Services

55 In the Land of the Blind

The one-eyed man is king. It has been my experience that when we deal with some of the softer, more ambiguous sides of business (strategy, alliances, people, customer needs) we often shy away from measuring inputs, activities, and outcomes because of the inherent ambiguity of some of the associated issues. In particular, I have often seen organizations essentially throw up their hands and omit measuring any of these items (inputs, activities and outcomes) when they realize that they can only obtain a partial picture owing to the difficulty and expense of data collection or because they lack confidence in what is actually being reported. However, I have always found that it is better to have a partial picture that is shared with all affected parties than to have no information at all. I normally break the issue into two categories: that which can be most easily and factually measured (objective) and that which may be so difficult or expensive to measure that it warrants relying on (cheaper and faster) subjective measures and assessments. One example – I once was tasked with transforming a business unit with flat growth and losses that operated in a rapidly growing market. A quick initial assessment indicated that we had good people with a strong culture but they were having difficulty understanding the actual execution of some of the core business strategies. We could look forward to rapid growth once they were coached into more effective execution, but our risk was that we might lose a good number of excellent performers

Performance measures should contain both objective and subjective components.

as we rapidly added headcount and potentially diluted the culture that they all valued. We implemented a performance mechanism that applied both objective and subjective measures in each category (inputs, activities and outcomes). We had the strongest objective measurement in the outcomes, about equal on the inputs and a majority of subjective measures in the activities category. None-the-less, by having standard criteria openly available to all parties we were able to significantly tighten up execution. With improved execution came profitability, revenue growth and headcount growth. The old guard, rather than being threatened, became the keepers of the measurement flame, constantly striving to improve overall measurement, better align it with strategies and execution, and holding the line for all parties against those measures. Unplanned turnover was exceedingly low and we quadrupled headcount in the space of three years with no significant erosion of the successful cultural components of the organization. We were far better off having partial measurement of soft issues in which everybody had a say in both creation and execution than having to rely on gut instinct and decision making by management fiat.

Charles Bayless

56 Application Software Selection

The first steps to any software selection should involve getting comprehensive business requirements from stakeholders and users. Once this data has been compiled and organized, it is best to search the market and references for vendors. After the vendors have been selected, each should demonstrate their abilities to accommodate the requirements dictated by stakeholders and users (first, via RFP, then after that list has been narrowed by Conference Room Pilot).

Once this is complete, the functional data should be tied to other data (company history, feasibility, price, etc.) to determine the best fit.

Doug Richards, Director of Professional Services, QuickArrow

57 Learning Good Habits at an Early Age

Focus on project and customer profitability, not just business unit P&L. The ability to look at project and customer profitability drives so many critical decisions made in an account from how to price services to how to handle discussions around concessions. Most savvy procurement departments will have this information. Not having this information puts you at a disadvantage in any negotiation.

Establish P&L accountability for all revenue forecasting within your delivery organization. Too often organizations try to split revenue forecasting responsibility between sales and delivery (i.e., delivery forecasts large project- based revenue streams while sales forecasts staff augmentation/smaller project work and "book/burn" within the quarter). Not only does this approach not work because there is no clear accountability, but the sales team often confuses bookings with burn and is often too optimistic about the ability to convert bookings to revenue in the quarter.

> 🕮 **Always stay focused on good business practices.**

Establish a strong operations team. While it is always a difficult decision to add non-billable resources to a consulting organization, a small group of highly talented resources will ensure process consistency and offload back office tasks from your prized billable resources. I also think it is a great approach to make ops roles rotational. This approach gives road warriors an opportunity to get off the road for a tour of duty and it ensures that your ops team is always in touch with the business and what is going on in the trenches.

Establish a Services Marketing and R&D team. Consulting is a unique profession in that, whether you are a part of a large software company or a pure consulting firm, you are responsible for building, marketing, selling and delivering your "product", i.e., your people and service offerings. Ironically, many consulting organizations overlook the marketing component. Again, it is always difficult to add non-billable resources to a consulting organization. However, road warriors typically have just enough hours in the week to do their client-facing and administrative work. They don't have time to answer questions like "How can we remain relevant as a consulting organization? How can we package our intellectual property as a competitive advantage? What are our highest margin offerings and how do we sell more of them?" Having a small team of professionals to focus on these questions ensures that your organization will continue to position and sell value-add, relevant, high-margin services that address the changing demands of your market segment.

Jason Blessing, General Manager, Taleo Business Edition

58 Contingency Planning

Rare is the project or engagement that goes as hoped for or as contracted. The consequences often are adverse economic impact, poor client relations and a discouraged customer and consulting team. Undesirable outcomes can be minimized by embracing a contingency or 'what if?' mentality.

A certain amount of paranoia is healthy in project planners and managers. Worry, to a degree, is a good thing. It is difficult to anticipate every turn during an engagement. Participants often discover obstacles and misunderstandings of scope, process and other conditions which hinder successful engagement completion. Engagement success often depends on how one handles the 'surprises'.

Think about "Plan B" because "Plan A" will not go exactly as expected.

Every planner and manager needs to sit down with the engagement plan before and <u>*after*</u> it has been accepted and review it for potential gotcha's. Doing this is as important as task definition, team selection, pricing and scheduling. Rank, but don't limit your assessment to the obvious hard-spots. Don't discard a potential concern just because it's unlikely.

Look at all the tasks for clarity and difficulty and consider what you'll do if you hit a bump. For example, look at the engagement staff, theirs and yours, and plot what you'll do if you lose key team members during the engagement. Another example, examine inter-group dependencies and the scenarios in which they interact. What are potential alternatives if things don't work – the software doesn't work as advertised, the companion supplier or customer/engagement team lack the needed skills, or go-forward decisions are delayed? Examine all the things for which your knowledge or experience is limited as well as 'weak spots' in the plan and make written and mental notes on how you'll address issues that threaten engagement performance.

Things go wrong. Having a plan 'B' before problems arise is essential. Anticipate. Don't wait until there's a problem. Focus on those things that have the potential for 'going south' to ensure a good outcome.

Jim Wallace, VP, eReplenishment.com

59 Defining Business Value

My favorite tip, which has been most important for me either as an external consultant or as an internal executive trying to validate a system 'buy' is the following:

The "Value" of a project is positively impacted by Quality and Service Delivered and is negatively impacted by Cost and Time. Every metric of quantifiable value can be defined by these relationships.

The formula "Value = (Quality * Service)/(Cost * Time)" expresses this concept. The formula probably needs some weighting factors to make it a truly accurate numeric formula, but we will use this formula in this discussion.

The Value of each project 'improvement', (for example, Time to Market for software development) can be expressed using these relationships. Thus, if we assume that the Quality and Service components will remain the same, the Value of an accelerated Time to Market is usually negatively impacted by an increase in cost, and it is positively impacted by the decrease in time. If more value is added by the decrease in time than is subtracted by the increase in cost, then positive value is attained. In this example, the increase in cost may come from increased headcount, multiple shifts of developers, on-site QA, etc.

Applying this equation to the Value of offshore development, we can see that the value will be positive if we are able to hold Quality, Service and Time the same, and if we are able to decrease the overall Cost of a project. Some factors that enter into this evaluation are:

Mix onshore and offshore resources to reduce headcount expense, reduce average cost of headcount, and reduce time to develop. Add increased overhead for collaborative management of remote development site to hold Quality 'neutral'. Add increased QA resources to hold Quality 'neutral'. Add additional hardware and software. Add bandwidth to manage change and version control to affect smooth hand-off from one site to the other to hold Quality 'neutral'. Add increased effort to document Requirements through Test and Acceptance to ensure communication and hold Quality 'neutral'. Hold 'time' to plan 'neutral'.

Four key parameters - Quality, Services Delivered, Cost and Time - can be used to quantify the value of almost any project.

A classic application of the formula pertains to the Value of improving Quality in a product or service. Usually improved Quality implies improved Service, increased short-term Cost and increased time in the short term to deliver the product or service. The true Value of improved quality lies in the long-term values that are factored into the formula.

Assessing the Value of Quality improvement is actually quite complicated. First a definition of the targeted Quality must be defined and agreed upon. For example for a Software Application one might choose "Reduce the number of 'business down' defects to zero" for each release. For many companies this increase in Quality to achieve 'positive' Value will require far more 'cost' and 'time' to achieve and may not be economically feasible but still requires investigation. Other considerations include:

Extensive Requirements through Release definition and documentation (Cost up)

Increases to not only testing time but also investment to complete (if there is such a thing)

Regression and business case testing (Time and Cost up)

By the time a company gets to this point of Quality perfection, the competition is usually two or three releases ahead and the Value will be negative - except in the case where a zero defect product is part of the necessary cost of doing business!

The overall point is that selling a solution should always incorporate rational thought somewhere in the proposal for a positive Value outcome and should be supported by an assessment of the quantifiable impacts to each of the four components of Value.

Bill Marshall, Owner, Marshall Management Consulting

60 PSA Systems and Shining a Lantern

One of my favorite business books is actually a book on politics. Before he found success on a cable television, Chris Matthews wrote "Hardball," which provides valuable insights into how to manage a complex high-cost organization. Chris's basic thesis is that you can "shine a lantern" on a problem and turn your challenges into strengths. Since it's a political book, he gives examples of how politicians do this all the time. Like politics, running a services firm requires enormous amounts of finesse and organization. PSA systems allow you to shine a light on your business in ways that were previously impossible.

Our company provides a great example. When we made the decision to hire a large number of expensive consultants, our board was naturally skeptical. Explaining the business rationale—that we needed highly trained people to implement systems and provide business process consulting to our clients—is something that we could do easily, but the board still remained skeptical. What finally convinced them were the detailed metrics of utilization and profitability. Using PSA to shine a lantern on our business showed the concrete financial benefits of our plan. When presented with these facts, the board's resistance dropped and we were given the green light for our plan.

Morris Panner, CEO, OpenAir

61 Centralized Resource Management

The most efficient Resource Management model will always be a Centralized one. The nature of Resource Management is that it requires the give-and-take of evaluating customer needs, customer expectations, and opportunity cost and balancing them against each other. That process involves communication with multiple groups. Centralizing the communication flow and decision making eliminates iterative and redundant communication channels.

While this is a broad statement, there is a scenario in which decentralizing Resource Management makes more sense: the inability (either by distance, cost or knowledge) to share resources between groups. In this case, separate Resource Management "centers" should be created and, ideally, those should function with a Centralized model within their own boundaries.

📖 **Centralized Resource Management is always more efficient than decentralized.**

Doug Richards, Director of Professional Services, QuickArrow

62 Timecards for Everyone

As a business operations manager for professional services, I am responsible for timely collection of weekly timecards. Unfortunately, engineers do not like to enter timecards. I have found it is best to address this head-on by requiring everyone, including all managers and executives, to enter timecards every week. This has several advantages:

- Makes monitoring COMPLIANCE much easier
- ELIMINATES the "us" versus "them" discussion between individual contributors and management
- CREATES opportunities for managers to charge time to projects

Glenda Aune

63 Cleaning Up Expense Management

We were having trouble with discretionary non-billable expense. Every dollar spent for non-billable travel, cell phones, blackberries, etc. was negatively impacting our margin.

We set out on a multi-step recovery plan:

- Conducted an in-depth analysis of all non-billable expense.
- Created a summary report by person (including managers) of their non-billable expense by month by category. The most dramatic finding was that several managers were spending over $3K per month for multiple cell phones, blackberries and PDAs and over $10K per quarter on non-billable travel and other expenses.
- Created a "get well" non-billable expense plan for the whole organization which included:

> **Every dollar spent for non-billable travel, cell phones, BlackBerries etc. can negatively impact margin.**

- With IT, developed a comprehensive telecommunications plan which included multiple devices, international calling and additional minutes for those who required it. We also standardized on the covered devices – moving the heavy travellers to blackberry phones to reduce excessive hotel internet charges.
- Changed our air travel policy to include efares through low-cost internet travel companies in addition to our corporate carriers and travel agency. Created an unwritten policy that all internal meetings requiring airfare had to be scheduled 2 weeks in advance to get the lowest air fares.
- Discontinued using "corporate" credit cards – required all employees to use individual business credit cards with weekly expense report submission. This turned out to be a big area for abuse and excess travel charges.

- Started publishing monthly non-billable expense reports by employee by manager. These reports immediately highlighted the "big spenders" and put pressure to get in-line.
- Every team was given a non-billable expense target of $2500 per employee per quarter. This provided an incentive to ensure all billable employees were accurately submitting rebillable client expenses and to more carefully plan non-billable trips for business development.
- Created a global expense account and budget for internal training held by the Global Readiness manager. She was responsible for creating the global employee training plan and curriculum. Once she had a budget for all internal training she was able to negotiate the best rates, venues, etc. for internal training – greatly improving the quality of training while reducing the cost.
- Worldwide Communication – included a description of the problem, the effects, and the "get well" plan in the worldwide quarterly "All Hands" calls. This allowed all employees to understand and internalize how they could directly improve margin.

By focusing on the issue and creating a "get well" plan that all employees could understand and embrace, non-billable expenses were dramatically reduced.

Jeanne Urich, Management Consultant, Adexta

64 Revenue Recognition and Invoicing

We ran into a situation one time when we crafted a statement of work based upon a time and materials basis with a not-to-exceed cap. This was for a new service offering, so we knew there was a probability that we would potentially hit the cap, but would consider it an investment that would allow us to scope, estimate and contract more accurately in the future.

The challenge came several months into the contract....we had been billing purely based upon a monthly T&M basis. The customer was quickly processing our invoices and remitting payment. So there were no issues with the quality of delivery, invoice or payment. The challenge was with the dreaded words we all fear: "revenue recognition".

We had been recognizing the revenue every month based upon our total T&M invoice. The project team knew they were going to go over budget, and were justified given that they had corporate support for this "early adopter" project. True, they had support to go over the not-to-exceed cap, but no one ever informed the Finance organization, who was recognizing revenue on a monthly basis.

Sure enough, we hit the cap later and Finance highlighted the fact that we had hours over our cap and assumed the project was complete. We worked with the project team and found out that the project was only approximately 70% of the way done. We learned at that point in time that we should have treated this project as a fixed fee and recognize revenue on a "percent complete" basis all along instead of standard T&M. Trouble was that we had no idea what the total hours would be until well into the project – UH OH!

Make sure your Finance department reviews customer contracts to avoid revenue recognition issues.

Finance immediately put revenue recognition on hold for this project, which was extremely painful and required a letter to the auditors. We then did not recognize revenue until we received final project sign-off, meaning we were working a sizeable number of hours that we couldn't recognize.

Lesson learned...have Finance review any non-standard deal structure, get Finance's approval, and begin the project under the correct accounting principle. If you don't know the percent complete early in the project, it's better to be conservative and recognize less in the beginning than to get into a situation where you run into revenue recognition issues later and have to have a tough talk with your CFO and auditors!

Derek Wolf, VP, Services Sales, Taleo

65 Managing Small T&M Projects

In deploying software or executing a change project of any size, customers will naturally ask – "How much will it cost to implement this system?" Many customers realize that given the uncertainties that exist before the project starts, your estimate is only that, an estimate. But some will take your estimate as an expectation of their final cost, and this can become especially difficult later in the project if a sponsor holds this assumption. Of course, even with a detailed knowledge of the scope, the effort involved in successfully achieving the project goals is critically dependent on a number of factors unknown to you when estimating:

> 🕮 **Continually let your team and the client know 'how much gas is left in the tank'.**

- The client's technical skills and infrastructure to adopt the new solution
- Whether their organization and processes have been appropriately defined and are even compatible with the solution to be implemented
- Whether the system will actually be implemented in the way you and the client first assumed – scope creep is the biggest single cause of project overruns
- Whether the schedule of the client's key team members allows them to focus on the implementation, and
- Whether turnover in the client organization will require restarts and rework.

While a large project can adopt an implementation approach with discrete phases, detailed tracking & reporting, and change control mechanisms, on small projects this level of management is not always viable. However, it is essential to keep the customer apprised of overall percentage progress, milestones accomplished and especially the cumulative spend against the total estimated budget. While it may be onerous to track at a detailed level, a simple cumulative total and estimate to complete lets your team and the client know "how much gas is left in the tank", and whether you can make it together to your destination!

It's also important to keep the client informed of status early and with reasonable frequency, even on the smallest of projects. While no-one likes to hear bad news, early communication makes it easier to either take corrective action to avoid repeating the problems, or to justify additional funding. Conversely, if the project is ahead of schedule the client may be happy to increase scope to make use of committed budget, and perhaps to avoid compromises they thought may be necessary in the implementation.

Richard Hayden, VP, Unanet Technologies

66 Support for New Systems

In my first job as a business operations manager, we implemented SAP Project Accounting. The system was installed. Everyone was trained. The consultants who led the implementation were gone. And here's what happened.

The first quarter that we used the system for revenue forecasting, we also collected weekly forecasts from the managers (Excel spreadsheets). When we compared the SAP data to the Excel spreadsheets, the total forecast was close but the individual project forecasts were completely different.

Make sure to have appropriate IT support in place to support your PS business.

When we asked a few managers if they could explain the differences, they told us not to worry because forecasting is an art, some projects will be a little over and some will be a little under. The closer we got to the end of the quarter, the larger the gap became between the SAP data and the weekly forecasts submitted by the managers. And then it became obvious – the project managers had entered data into the SAP system during training (months earlier) and had never updated the project data because they did not know how to use the new system. In fact, most of them did not understand project accounting and did not know they were expected to update the system because they were submitting their forecasts to their managers. We immediately eliminated the use of Excel spreadsheets for forecasting and required everyone to use SAP. And, we put SAP analysts (experts in using the system) in place to support the project managers. The analysts held their hands to ensure new projects were set up correctly and all projects were updated so that they generated revenue as expected. We continued this support even after project managers learned to use the system because project accounting is complex and project managers, especially new ones, need support.

Unfortunately this is not a unique experience. I have seen this happen in other organizations. My advice to anyone implementing new systems, especially project accounting, is to put a good support structure in place.

Glenda Aune

67 PS Professionals and Utilization

I recently joined a new firm through an acquisition transaction. I quickly learned that the other members of our management team had diverse backgrounds from a number of different professional services (PS) organizations. One of our initial challenges as a team was to make sure we were speaking the same language when we viewed the metrics of running our business. One of the metrics that caused some good discussion was utilization.

Utilization is important to PS professionals as it describes how well the firm is keeping available resources working on projects. PS companies are only profitable if their resources are generating more revenue than they cost, and because they are human resources they don't typically generate revenue unless they are working on customer-facing revenue generating activity. Utilization can be used to measure historical performance and can also be used as a forecasting tool. Utilization is typically expressed as a percentage of how much time a PS professional is working on projects versus

> **Utilization is key to understanding how well a PS business is running.**

how much time is available to work on projects. That is where the discussion became complicated among our management team.

We quickly learned that the number of hours that someone is working on projects is more complex than it appears. Should internal projects be counted in those hours, or only external, client-facing, revenue-generating projects? What about available hours? Should we include holidays, weekends, or other hours where we really don't expect our staff to be working, but in theory are times that are available to work? And then vacation comes in – should it impact the numerator or the denominator?

Our firm considered multiple utilization metrics, but the one we look at most is (client hours + internal project hours)/(40 hours per week – company holiday – vacation). This metric helps us understand how "hot" we are running. You don't necessarily have to use this as your metric, but you should look at utilization and determine how you want to measure your productivity and make sure everyone on your management team and staff are aligned with it.

Tom Keuten, Principal, Pariveda Solutions

68 Dynamic Knowledge Management

Like most other professional services organizations, a great deal of useful knowledge and experience is locked up inside our people's heads. We strive to write white papers, add best practice engagement documents to our methodology, develop new training, etc. Alas, these strategies help but are not enough. When a new person comes into the organization or if we lose a really experienced professional, the need to transfer knowledge into or out of someone is hit or miss. Also, we found that our best people were constantly asked the same questions over and over again as new people either joined or others didn't remember to check the past email chain or discussion.

A good knowledge portal provides great leverage.

Therefore, we decided to capture knowledge in a different way. We utilize a knowledge portal that front-ends a discussion board. When anyone in our practice has a question for other professionals, wants to share a best practice or lesson learned, or provides something that doesn't warrant a formal document, they enter it on the portal. Once the comment is posted, the technology we utilize creates tags to enable others to search for it in the future and monitor topics of interest. When people respond to the comment, they add new tags if appropriate further enhancing its usability; they also vote on the usefulness of the entry through a simple click. The result of this process is the really good bits of knowledge float to the top of the pile where others can easily find them. This process allows us to gather ideas and practices on a real-time basis that can be easily found through the use of tagging and searching.

One of the critical success factors for using a system like this is changing the culture of how people work. Before using this system, we exchanged knowledge like everyone else; through the use of "Reply All" emails, Instant Messaging our colleagues, or hallway conversations. We (the management team) encourage people to use the tool instead of lapsing into old habits. If we see someone emailing something that is better suited for the portal, we reply "Take it to the board."

The combination of a powerful technology, cultural change, and working differently allows us to build a knowledge base that is constantly refreshed and expanded as people do their day-to-day work. It also serves as a source for the other things we all like to do like white papers, best practice documents, and new training.

Jason Rothbart, VP, Professional Services, newScale

69 Project Staffing is a Collaborative Process

In the late 1990s I was working for a hugely successful consulting company. In less than a decade, we had grown from a handful of local offices to a nationwide force of thousands. As we'd grown, our staffing process had evolved from a local operation, handled separately by each office, to a national process. The shift had not gone smoothly.

All we wanted was to put the right people with the right skills in the right place at the right time. But despite our best efforts, the staffing experience had become a chaotic free-for-all. No one was happy.

Even under the best conditions, it isn't easy to staff professional services projects to satisfy everyone. Demand seldom matches supply. Project leaders compete for the best talent. Consultants compete for the best projects. Everyone jockeys for advantage.

Our national staffing process seemed to make sense, on paper. Project leaders had to submit written requests to the staffing team. The staffing team did their best to fill these "requisitions" based on rules about which types of requests had priority. But project leaders weren't getting the people they needed, and consultants were not getting assignments that fit them. In their frustration, everyone tried to bypass the staffing team and make their own arrangements, which just made the situation more chaotic.

As we began to rethink the process, one of our Staffing Specialists drew the picture in Figure 1. She pointed out that we were thinking in terms of a "requisition model." Everything about our process seemed to reflect a view that consultants were spare parts who could be boxed up and shipped out via next-day air.

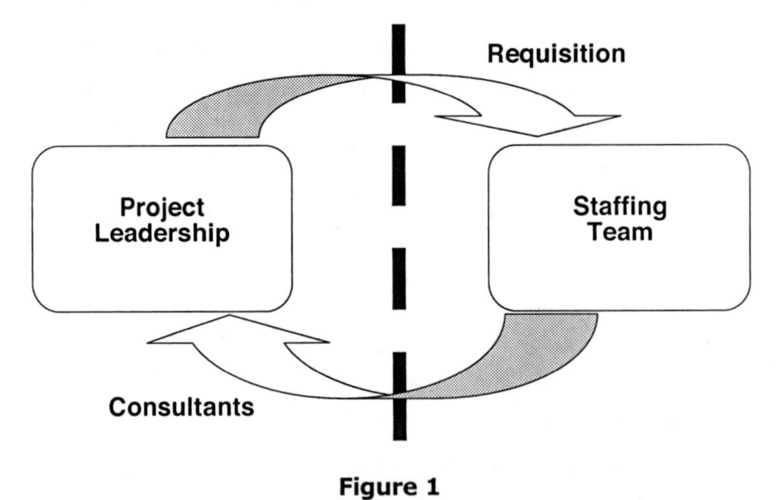

Figure 1

She had our attention. We realized that a requisition process might work if we were selling a simple, commodity service, and we had an unlimited supply of people with the required skills. But that's not the kind of business we were in. Our services weren't simple, and we didn't have an unlimited supply of consultants. What's more, if we were temporarily "out of stock" we couldn't just put a staffing requisition on back-order and ship in a week when the "product" came in.

So we faced facts, and created a more realistic model of how project staffing really worked for us. In our business, we realized, staffing required a high degree of partnership between project leaders and staffing specialists. The partnership had to be an ongoing dialog, not a one-time interaction.

Figure 2 shows the new model we created. Project leaders worked closely with the staffing team, so that staffing was a shared process. They would keep staffers informed about their upcoming needs, which they tracked in project-pricing and costing spreadsheets, and staffers would keep the project leaders informed about staff availability, which shifted daily. Since all the factors were constantly in flux, they would work together to explore options right up to the time a decision had to be made.

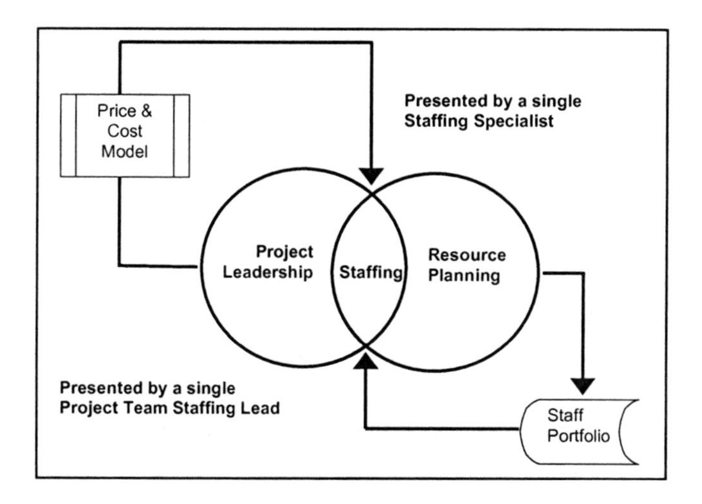

Figure 2

But we realized we couldn't have several people on a project team interacting with several members of the staffing team. That would take us right back to chaos. So we established a simple rule: "one decision, made collectively, but communicated with one voice." Only one Staffing

Lead per team would coordinate staffing needs with the staffing team, and only one Staffing Specialist would coordinate with each project team. Only one person – the Staffing Specialist – would notify consultants of staffing decisions.

"One decision, made collectively, then communicated with one voice." That was the simple idea from which a successful new process emerged. Of course, we still had to have guidelines for deciding which openings would get priority, and guidelines for respecting the preferences of individual consultants, and a way to resolve disputes quickly and fairly. But our process was no longer driven and dominated by these rules. It was driven increasingly by teamwork and collaboration. As the level of teamwork went up, the number of disputes quickly decreased.

Perhaps there are no new lessons in this story. But for us there were several important reminders of old lessons we'd forgotten. Like "people aren't widgets." And "everyone wants a say in their own destiny." And "rules are no substitute for communication."

Most of all, we learned that a business process is fundamentally a conversation. If your process isn't working, that's a sign that important conversations aren't taking place. We learned that if we create the space for these missing conversations, the process will pretty much heal itself.

Stuart Scott, CEO, Guinnen MacRath LLC

70 The Benefits of Reviewing Your Call Center Database

At a small software company, while doing a review of our Customer Service Database, we noticed in addition to the customary issues that one could expect to find such as limited management visibility and poor reporting tools there were also a large number of calls that were wasting both the call center and the customer's time. Customers were frustrated with the fact that they had high volumes of "how to "questions that could have been averted with

Review call center operations for clues about how to better run your business.

sufficient training and focused service offerings. In addition, the Call Center staff was becoming worn out by the volume and nature of the questions.

We implemented new call center software that resolved the reporting and visibility issues immediately, and then focused our efforts on the volume of calls. By launching a series of improvements to the education, documentation, and professional services offerings we were able to provide better information to our customers, which reduced the need for repetitive call-ins.

On average, our call volume dropped by 50% and we were able to more than double the number of customers while our Call Center staff remained the same size. Morale within the Center improved as the staff no longer felt that they were wasting time on repetitive tasks. Our customer satisfaction rates increased dramatically as we were now better equipped to address any issues that arose. Subsequently, our PS revenues also increased as customers purchased the additional "packaged services" that Professional Services was now able to offer.

Scott Fletcher, Director, InfoMentis, Inc.

4. Methodology

This chapter covers topics such as expectation setting, establishing acceptance criteria, requirements gathering, project management and effective use of templates.

"Either lead, follow, or get out of the way.
But never try to do all three at the same time!"

71 Communication is Key in Project Management

Documentation for the PMI certification testing process states that one of the project manager's most important skills is communication. It is estimated that an effective project manager spends about 90% of his or her time communicating, and fully 50% of that time is spent communicating within the project team. While reviewing the lessons learned from our implementations we have found that the vast majority, if not all, of the negative variances encountered with our projects have a common root cause. You guessed it – lack of timely and accurate communication both with the clients and within the internal project team. We have taken several steps to rectify this:

Every high-level project plan includes quality planning documentation which documents the client's expectations, business needs to implement our software and details on any item which is not "out-of-the-box" and/or departs from our standard processes and procedures. This documentation is used to communicate to the project team the bottom line objectives of the project from the client's perspective.

Every project plan should include a communications plan with details regarding who, what and when.

Every project plan, no matter what the size of the project, must include a communications plan with detail including who, what, and when. The project manager can then focus on the execution of the communications plan to manage both the client and the project teams as his/her first priority. This process has minimized surprises and unexpected events. The client knows when and how the project status is going to be communicated.

Every project plan now includes not only duration and work for our efforts but also an estimate for the time our client's internal staff is expected to spend on project steps. This step has really helped set the client's expectations of what will be expected from them and when it is necessary to accomplish the tasks. In fact, the project manager's job has gotten easier since we have found that our clients proactively manage their resources to our plan.

Most phases of our original projects did not explicitly state the milestones and deliverables but simply stated what tasks were being performed with the name of the phases being an implied milestone and deliverable. Every project plan now has one or more deliverables and milestones explicitly stated. The client's acceptance of the phase is one of those milestones. This addition has everyone on the project team focused on the end result of the phase, not just on the tasks to be performed. The status of the deliverables and milestones are also incorporated into the communication plan, and this has worked extremely well.

While there are additional communications planning items, these are the items we have found most useful to increase our clients' satisfaction in improving our delivery time and margins.

Harry Roberts

72 Process Assessment

In a previous role as VP of Consulting I was challenged with turning around an ailing consulting organization and building a profitable service business in a traditional box product company that had relied for over 20 years on its reseller network to deliver minimal customer training and very basic consulting. The company had released a portfolio of "solutions" that were considerably more complex to implement than their traditional product lines and was finding those solutions both hard to sell and difficult to implement using their VAR network. To a service professional it was obvious they were lacking the full service offering that customers required to be successful with the solutions, and the skills required were, for the most part, not available from their traditional sales channel. The only way they could build customer confidence to the level required was to show the customer both the value of the solution and also HOW they could implement successfully.

Effective assessment builds good credibility.

We did a multitude of changes like aligning the organizations to industry verticals, hiring the correct skillsets, building a strong management team, restructuring the bonus plans, building relationships with the VARs, etc. --- most of which I do not want to focus on here (I just don't want to oversimplify the amount of change required to successfully make this work). I do want to focus on a simple methodology change that we implemented to assist the sales team and make customers aware of the value of the solution and also build the confidence required for them to understand "why us". We introduced a package service called a "Process Assessment". The activity was placed at the front of our implementation methodology and was built into the sales methodology as well, as a key step to closing the "deal".

The package was a fixed-price, fixed-scope service with pre-defined templates, processes and deliverables. The price was set to establish the value of the service, but we were very flexible when working with a customer on the actual price, or in working out a contingent arrangement (for example, the price was $10,000 plus expenses but the $10,000 fee was applied to the future implementation services if the customer moved forward with the deal). Customers generally don't value free services so if we decided to waive the fee, we still presented the customer with a zero-balance invoice. The service was delivered by a very senior project/engagement manager and possibly involved other consultants if specific product and/or process knowledge were required. We always required a customer counterpart or even a small project team to work with our team. The results were then viewed as "joint" findings and were much more credible.

The assessment consisted of 1-2 days on-site working with the team, 2-3 days of write-up and review, then ended with a joint presentation to the project sponsors. The team answered 5 questions:

1. What is your current process? ("as is" state)
2. What are your business goals?
3. What are the roadblocks to accomplishing your goals?
4. What solutions are available to overcome these business challenges? ("to be" state)
5. What value will the solutions return once implemented (return on investment)?

The final deliverable took the form of a PowerPoint presentation and summarized the five questions. The presentation included a solution map that graphically illustrated the future state. The team presented the findings to the project sponsors and our account manager. The deliverable formed the basis for a business case to internally justify the project. More often than not the presentation was actually delivered by one of the customer team members with our consultant there to answer questions and support the team (again, the information is much more credible when it comes from the customer's own employees). This delivery set up the next step, building a formal proposal and (if we did our job right) moving forward with the implementation.

Michael Fauscette, VP, Software Applications Research, IDC

73 SOW Automation

Most SOWs are a combination of company standards (business terms, contractual language) + scope description + resources + rates + timelines. Generating this document by cutting and pasting leads to errors and can take a bit of time as you hunt for all the pieces and get inputs and reviews from other people. You can reduce errors and save significant time and resources if you take the time to automate building the SOW.

> **SOW automation builds credibility and makes everybody's job easier.**

Using Microsoft Word and VBA create a SOW that is consistent with your company's legal and business terms, yet customized to the client. You can take this one step further by automatically producing the SOW along with change bars on the client-specific items for your lawyer, a summary document for Finance, and a "burn rate" spreadsheet report for the project manager.

Structure the work so each piece of the document can be created in separate input documents that each department can own -- Legal, Finance, Consulting Management. Thus, your initial draft will be pre-approved by all parties and have everything they need to do their jobs. As business evolves, your legal personnel can edit their "inputs", finance personnel can keep their text up to date and you always produce a first draft that is consistent with your business plan.

This also builds a large amount of credibility with the client when 15 minutes after you finish meeting you produce a draft document based on your discussions for your client's review.

Karl M. Waldman

74 Keys for Managing Project Estimates

I've been responsible for producing a lot of estimates over the past 10 years. It is one of the most stressful times in the entire project for everyone involved. My firm builds custom web-based software for our clients, a process fraught with risks, uncertainty, and dreaded unknown-unknowns. Estimating is hard. But our clients, much like your clients, don't really care how hard it is to produce an estimate. All they want to know is, "How long is it going to take and how much is it going to cost?"

> **Credible estimates result from following a well-designed process.**

So with that in mind, here are some tips to help produce better estimates and manage risk:

Aim for accuracy, not precision. The subtle difference between accuracy and precision is the most overlooked aspect of estimation. Customers ask "How much is my project going to cost?" and the gut reaction is to come back with a single number. Single numbers (like the number $17,000) are precise. They are exact. But they might not be accurate. Accuracy is all about how close your number is to the final number. And accuracy at the start of a project is difficult to achieve due to the large amount of uncertainty of what is going to be implemented.

So to achieve accuracy, expect a range. Between $10,000 and $30,000 is accurate when the final value is $17,000. It may not be precise, but when faced with uncertainty around precision, an accurate range of $10,000 to $30,000 is better than an over-inflated, but precise, single number of $28,000 if the final amount is really $17,000.

Provide as much detail as possible. More often than not, a brief, one-page overview of a software application is not enough to provide a good estimate. The more detail the better. If a potential client can provide a specification document, sample mockup screens, technical architecture or use-case scenarios; all of these project deliverables shed light into the mystery of what you're trying to build. The more of this material a developer has access to, the better informed they are. The better informed they are, the more likely the chances are they will be able to provide an estimate that accurately reflects the effort required to build your final product.

Invest in up-front analysis work. Don't have the detail? Don't have a 50 page spec and a stack of 85 wireframes that describe the entire application? Prepare to invest in some up-front analysis and design work. Often, we'll engage a client in up-front analysis and design work and once we're done, we'll fix-price estimate the rest of the project. The client gets useful design documents that accurately describe the system, we get a much better understanding of what it's going to do, and we're now able to produce valid estimates for the rest of the development.

Don't play the guessing game. At some point every software professional will trot out the "iron triangle" of constraints: features, cost, and schedule. That never seems to stop the requests for the most features for the least cost in the shortest time possible.

The cost corner of the triangle is a very important one, and is often known, but hidden during the estimating process. Don't make the developer guess. The cost anchor on the triangle is just as important as the features you want or how long we have to build them. If your budget to finish your bathroom is $5,000, not $20,000, then different decisions will be made. Bye-bye marble countertops, hello laminate!

Pick a corner. How flexible are your features? Willing to get rid of a few? How about the timeline? Is that September date really crucial? And the budget... any contingency built into it? Knowing your degree of freedom for each of the corners of the "features, cost, schedule triangle" is crucial. Estimation is a process of negotiation and knowing where you stand firm and where you have flexibility is important to determine and communicate.

Iterate your estimates. Not willing to invest in some "design up front" to come up with your fixed-price estimate at the start of the project? Then prepare yourself to forge ahead and live with some uncertainty at the start, but expect ranges of increasing accuracy as the project moves along. Iterative estimation incorporates learning along the way, increasing accuracy as it goes forward, with the ranges becoming closer and closer.

Targets vs. estimates: understand the difference. Estimating is a bottom-up approach: on a feature-by-feature, screen-by-screen basis, how much effort will this take? Targeting takes the opposite, top-down approach — choose a desired end-point and work back from it (i.e., your budget of $100,000). But the bottom line is the same — your budget and features will often be at odds throughout the project. And there's no guarantee that your target of $100,000 and your project list of 258 features will match up nicely. For anyone that's built something before, software or otherwise, this will be no surprise.

In summary, estimating is tough. To achieve accuracy and precision requires a lot of hard work, both for those producing the estimate and those on the receiving end. It's an imperfect process and one that can have a huge impact on the life of your project if not done correctly. So give yourself some time, invest in up-front work, and be realistic. Your project will be better because of it.

Gordon Ross, VP/Partner, OpenRoad Communications

75 Up-Front Specification of UAT and Test Data Sets

Our experience is that securing project sign-off can be a major obstacle if the definition of success is not clearly stated near the beginning of the project.

It's always smart to ask the customer during requirements gathering how they would define success. We've found though that many customers have not thought seriously about the definition of success, or if they have, they do not have quantitative measures for success. If they have thought it through, the customer's definition of when the software is ready to deploy in production may be quite different than

> 🕮 **Project scope creep can be minimized by well thought out acceptance specs.**

ours (the vendor). Certainly with any software there are always further improvements that can be made, but many customers are looking for "perfection" at sign-off, and we've found this is only (if ever) attained after extended use of the application with continual modifications.

Our solution is to now require two pre-defined data sets which are representative of the customer's overall operations.

The first data set is relatively large and is used as our development and test data set. We build our custom solution on this data set. The second data set is smaller, and it is defined as the control data set. When we install the software to begin the UAT (user acceptance test), we use the control data set. If we are successful in meeting the pre-defined standards with this control data set, we have automatic agreement that the work will be signed off, and we can bill for our work. We agree to fix any serious problems (not cosmetic issues or feature enhancements) to make the results of operating on the control data set fully acceptable to the user.

This approach clearly defines the success criteria up-front and avoids alterations to the project scope due to new or unanticipated data.

Don Field, VP, Professional Services, Kofax Image Products

76 Gathering Business Requirements Effectively

Have you been in a situation where you had a challenge of obtaining consensus on your business requirements or design during a software application implementation involving a very diverse group of project team members?

One of the techniques we used was to establish "champions" or "business owners" for various groups so that the requirements were properly debated and analyzed within these groups and channeled to a smaller group of champions for finalization of the requirements or design. This way all members were enabled to have a voice and provide input as part of the process.

Use customer team champions to streamline the gathering of business requirements.

We also made it a point to close the loop by bringing the groups back for review and explaining to them how we came to the final positions. The net result of using this technique was that the final delivery of the project was a harmonized system that met the diverse requirements for a global project.

Peter Wong, Manager, Nextance Inc.

77 Use of Good Templates

As someone who has had responsibility for both management and delivery of enterprise application implementation and consulting services, the most valuable tools my team has are service delivery templates that provide a repeatable methodology for setting customer expectations and guiding service delivery. In project post mortems, lack of a template or lack of use of an available template more often than not is the root of a less than excellent customer experience.

Templates play an indispensable role from end to end including pre-sales discovery, project kickoff and planning, project requirements gathering as well as testing and delivery. A solid set of engagement lifecycle templates raises the overall quality of the team's deliverables, provides a solid foundation for incorporating Best Practices and Lessons Learned and also provides a vehicle for quickly ramping up new employees or partners.

Good templates save time and improve all aspects of project delivery.

Scott McCourt, Director of Consulting Services, Axeda Corp.

78 Setting Expectations Early On

In order to declare success in the PS or Operations environment it is critical that appropriate expectations are set as early in a project as possible, regardless of whether the expectations are what the customer wants to hear or not. It is a must to live in the realistic environments and stay away from only discussing what the customer wants to hear.

This approach allows for Services Professionals to build credibility and to have difficult conversations once, rather than multiple times, in an effort to cover up or explain why the expectations were not met.

Although customers may not seem as though they want to hear it then, it can be assured that it will be appreciated long term.

Micheal Eicher, Vice President of Professional Services, Paisley

79 Clearly Define Acceptance Criteria Up-front

You've probably heard the advice to "begin with the end in mind" applied to everything from choosing your life goals to creating a data model. Well, it's good advice when it comes to writing a statement of work or beginning a project, too. I've found that documenting well-defined acceptance criteria for a project up-front can be beneficial in many different ways.

First, having the conversation with the project sponsor about "what do you expect the outcome of this project to be?" can be enlightening. It is a good time to adjust any expectations that might be out of line with what your team can deliver. Trust me, realigning mis-set expectations only gets harder with each passing day.

Second, having clear goals for project acceptance provides a great scope management tool. When the more tactical customer team members come up with great idea after great idea of additional things to add to the project scope, you have a measuring stick - the acceptance criteria. If new items will get you closer to the goals for the project, consider them. If they only get you closer to some other unstated goal, no matter how noble that goal is, then be aggressive about keeping the items out of scope (or better yet, exercise the greatest tool of the services professional - the Change Order!)

> **Early setting of acceptance criteria contributes to smooth project execution.**

Last, but not least, you have a way to end the project. Believe it or not, that it not as easy as it sounds some times. With well-defined acceptance criteria, you know when you're done. You can ask the client for written acceptance. You can begin talking about future projects. Without well-defined goals for the project, the project "tail" can get very long. That's not good for fixed-bid or time-and-materials engagements when they run too long or over budget.

So, take the time up-front to be clear, through written documentation, with your project sponsor about what the specific acceptance criteria are for the engagement.

Dean M. Thomas, VP, Client Services, Merced Systems Inc.

80 Communication Plan for Project Governance

I have spent a considerable amount of time working on recovering projects which have gone bad. Invariably, a key factor behind this has been a breakdown in basic program governance procedures.

While the majority of projects will start out with a well accepted project methodology which includes the formulation of a Project Management Plan, a key component of this plan which is often overlooked, or not kept up-to-date, is the Communications Plan.

Know what your customer views as success.

In my experience, the Communications Plan is one of the key components in the Project Management Plan, as breakdown in communication is one of the most common causes of project failure. At a minimum, the Communications plan should include the following sections:

- Project team organization chart
- Formal communication channels – i.e., what are the normal lines of communication between the project team and the client team
- Issue management process
- Formal escalation process - both vendor and client teams
- Structure of the document management repository

- Document management register – this register is used to keep track of documents through the review process until they are signed off by the client as accepted
- Schedule of all regularly scheduled project meetings (e.g. Steering Committee, project review meetings, project team meetings). This schedule should list the purpose of the meeting, meeting frequency, attendees and chair. All meetings should have minutes recorded, and this schedule should include the list of persons to whom the minutes should be circulated.

Communicate often and well, and in accordance with a well-defined communication plan.

Kevin Hanvey, Executive Director, Taking Aim Pty. Ltd.

81 Success Criteria

Do you ever wonder what is most important to your customer and where you should focus your limited resources to have the maximum impact on customer satisfaction? Ask them! When assessing customer satisfaction it is important to understand the criteria that are most important to the customer and what will determine the customer's overall satisfaction with the services being delivered. At the start of a project, preferably in the sales cycle, ask the key project sponsors to pick 3 to 5 items from a pre-defined list that they feel are the most important to the success of their project. Examples include – scope management, on time, on budget, cultural fit, quality of deliverables, responsiveness, etc. At pre-defined intervals and/or key project milestones check the client's satisfaction against the selected performance criteria. Understanding what the client deems most important early on allows you to structure the project appropriately and focus your efforts on the items that will deliver the most value to your customer and also to you.

When assessing customer satisfaction it's important to understand the criteria that are most important to the customer.

Mark Rask, Services Director, Lawson Software

82 Project Management Assets, Guidelines and Tools

"What's your methodology?" "What level CMM are you?" "What's your change management process?" These are all questions that we answered every time we had a new project with a new customer. Why is it that every time we were getting ready to start a project, we always felt like we were getting ready from scratch? And for newly hired project managers, training was inconsistent and highly variable depending on the amount of free time available to their managers when they started.

We decided it was time to "stop and sharpen the saw" so we could gain efficiency and have more consistency. We spent time creating reusable assets that were template based. We created an inventory of approximately 30 documents that ranged in type from "education" documents we could give to prospective and new customers (such as a glossary of terms, delivery process overview, etc.) to delivery oriented documents for project costing, resource planning, and tracking. These templates also served as a great methodology "cookbook" that gave us a simple checklist-based process that was easy to follow.

Good documentation creates reusable assets.

Once we put the time into this effort, we found that maintenance of the materials was much easier, as the documents were centrally located (and not scattered all over individuals' computers). The efficiency gain we realized was immense. We had a consistent message, reusable assets, and a clear method to deliver the message. We were able to prepare for meetings faster and felt confident that the methodology we used was now precisely documented for our customers and employees.

The short message: Take the time to document what you do and create reusable assets.

The result: Great results, every time.

Steven Giangregorio, Professional Services/Operations Executive

83 Business Integration

Take a Business Integration approach to everything you do, both externally with your customers and projects, and internally with your Practice Management. Any business problem can be diagnosed by considering the Strategic, Process, Technology and People components. Most Professional Services folks use this approach for building methodology and running their customer projects, but this approach is equally valid and equally powerful for internal Practice Management areas. For example, Recruiting, Performance Reviews, Services Financial Management, Resource Management, etc. all require a strategy that is somewhat dictated by the size of your Services team, and the number of customers/projects you are managing. From the strategy, effective processes, tools and organization can be put in place. The Business Integration Model is an extremely powerful tool --- use it everywhere to manage your Services business.

Mark McKenzie

84 Requirements Gathering

As software experts in the field, our role is to determine requirements, scope the effort level, and set realistic expectations. The fit gap analysis is not only crucial to the success of any project, but is also the baseline and foundation on which a project is based. Too many times this is forgotten, and issues such as scope creep, misunderstandings, and too many change requests occur which ultimately lead to over-budgeted project costs and a late go-live date. Setting realistic expectations from the beginning and defining appropriate phases have been the paramount reasons for the successes I've been able to achieve at client sites. The soft skills and the relationships that are built are key to understanding customer needs and being able to successfully deliver projects.

Invest in a high quality fit-gap analysis.

Tejune Kang, President, Six Dimensions

85 Maximizing the Effectiveness of Project & Program Reviews

Everyone does project and program reviews and just about every project manager dislikes them. To make matters worse, most client personnel, both end user and IT, share that opinion. Yet we keep doing them and for good reason, when done correctly they are the single most effective technique to keep projects on track.

I have been involved in a management capacity with well over a hundred large-scale enterprise software projects over my career on both the IT and consulting side of the table. It took me a long time to discover a very simple technique that has dramatically improved the effectiveness of project reviews. The tip is so simple I'm almost embarrassed to share it but its effectiveness and ease of implementation makes it valuable.

When a new project is launched and the project schedule and governance are being established, I give the project manager one simple directive regarding project reviews: they must be scheduled on the same day of the week, at the same time each week, in the same conference room, with the same conference call-in number, the same attendees and the same agenda for the ENTIRE project.

> 🕮 **Schedule project reviews so that they are fixed on the schedules of all project team members.**

In addition, the meeting is put on everyone's schedule at the start of the project for the entire project. The frequency, weekly or biweekly, may be different from situation to situation, but the project review schedule is done ONCE and never changes. The same for steering committees or PMO reviews. I encourage the PM to keep the agenda VERY simple (what was accomplished in the last week, what will be accomplished next week, problems encountered, and financial status) and very straightforward.

This works for a number of pretty basic reasons:

- It makes it easy for the PM, they set it up once and then execute each week.
- It becomes routine and the attendees become comfortable with each other and the problem-resolution process.
- It forces regular and routine conversation on problems, and because of the frequency the problems are addressed when they are small and easier to correct (fire prevention vs. fire fighting).
- It provides a regular and frequent forum to raise issues and concerns, which promotes early discussion of problems well before they become potential career killers.
- The project reviews become more focused and time efficient as the project goes on.
- It provides senior management with a very quick and easy way to do an on the ground project health check.

Since beginning to use this technique the project managers who follow the structure religiously have had FAR greater success with substantially fewer project problems. Those that haven't had faced more aggravation, especially toward the end of their projects.

The essence of the tip is to make the EXECUTION simple, easy and relevant. My experience has told me that PMs overly complicate this process or simply do a poor job with project reviews. The end result is one we all know too well… surprises, affixing blame, budget overruns, etc. As some wise sage once said "Keep it simple".

Tom Minick, Independent Management Consultant

86 How to Describe the Change Order Process

When to issue a Change Order? This is an area where a Project Manager needs to walk a fine line between institutionalizing good project discipline versus becoming too rigid or inflexible with the customer. One can set the tone early on how the

SOW will be used as a guide and Change Orders may be used simply to clarify any ambiguities in the SOW. This is a particularly useful tactic if the customer is extremely sensitive to the term "increased scope."

Anonymous

87 File Naming Convention

When multiple people are involved in reviewing SOWs, contracts and other important documents, adopt a strict file naming convention. One good file naming convention entails ending the name of every document with an unambiguous date followed by a single sequencing character (for example 2006-10-24a). The sequencing character supports the fact that multiple versions of the document are sometimes generated within the same day.

Also establish a rule whereby each reviewer changes the file name by only changing the date or the sequencing character. Thus, if the reviewer receives a document named "Company A App B SOW 2006-10-24a.doc", then after reviewing the document on October 26th, the reviewer is expected to name the file as either:

📖 **Strong document naming conventions lead to improved operational clarity.**

"Company A App B SOW 2006-10-26a.doc" or "Company A App B SOW 2006-10-24b.doc".

Use of either of these names has the desirable result of guaranteeing that the character string at the end of the file name is always increasing in value, and hence it is unambiguous regarding which version of the file is the most current.

After establishing this file naming convention we noticed the following process improvements.

1. It was obvious which version of the file contained the most recently reviewed content.
2. The consistency of file naming was much appreciated both by internal organizations and by customers who were involved with the exchanging of files for review.

3. Customers and internal personnel were able to use a very efficient shorthand notation for referring to versions of documents. For example, we would refer to version "10-24b from Tom", rather than "the version that was edited yesterday by Tom after receiving the edits of Anne".

The bottom line was that "mental clutter" was avoided and lost time was minimized by the adoption of a strong document naming convention for PS documents that were touched by multiple persons.

Bill Morton, Vice President of Services, Acesis Inc.

88 Tools and Knowledge Sharing in a PSO

In PS organizations, one of the recurring difficulties is in maintaining consistent quality as your organization grows. Geographic separation, multiple teams working on multiple projects, combined with tight deadlines and a pressure to work on billable items, can lead to a rapidly growing organization with steadily decreasing efficiency. Teams do not always communicate with each other, and unless a framework is put in place to facilitate knowledge-sharing, time will be lost solving previously solved problems. I have seen even the sharpest teams perform unnecessary work, simply due to their unfamiliarity with past projects.

> **Thorough knowledge sharing enables scalability.**

Putting a knowledge-sharing framework in place is not necessarily expensive, and will pay for itself in terms of efficiency, increased capacity and customer satisfaction due to shorter delivery times and higher quality. I have had good success with the following tools:

Pre-project review with leaders: This is a means by which the team of a new project can enlist ideas from PS leadership. This could be a formal teleconference, or it could simply be an email that spells out the details or challenges of a new implementation. The important point is for the leadership team to be aware of what is being implemented, so they can offer relevant pointers from their experience.

Forums: A forum is a web site where team members can post help requests for issues. Other team members review and post responses. At first, it may be necessary to encourage participation, but eventually this will be unnecessary. Providing recognition for those who frequently help others will drive adoption. To be most useful, the forums should be divided into several categories and topics.

Knowledgebase: A knowledgebase is similar to a forum, except that instead of posting questions, useful articles are posted. As a team implements new reusable features, or develops expertise in a certain area, an article should be posted so that others can leverage that expertise. Team leaders should be diligent about recognizing potential topics in their current projects, and again, recognition of frequent contributors goes a long way to encourage adoption.

Periodic solution presentations: A monthly web conference provides a venue for a team to take pride in its delivery, as well as to share information about issues that were overcome, new tools and components that were developed, etc. Ideally, a checklist for the presentations should be developed to ensure the presentations fulfill their objectives. Another variation of this is for a team lead to send an email containing key information announcing the completion of a deployment.

Idea list for tools and documentation to help the organization: As new hires are trained, and as implementations are completed, deficiencies in your documentation, tools and training materials will be discovered. Create a forum area to list improvement suggestions and discussions. Leaders should periodically prioritize these items, assign ownership, and have them worked on during bench time. This will result in a gradual improvement of the practice.

Alex Carr, VP Raleigh Solution Center, Aprimo Inc.

5. Services Marketing

This chapter covers topics such as marketing tools, service packaging, lead generation, customer satisfaction and effective presentations.

"I gave a presentation today but I only pretended to know what I was talking about. Fortunately, my audience was only pretending to listen."

89 What Marketing Materials Do I Need?

Whenever I work with professional service organizations, the first item everyone wants is a datasheet or brochure. I tell people that is the last item they should want. I have never seen services sold by leaving behind a datasheet or brochure. However, it is the most requested and sometimes the only piece of marketing collateral a service organization will get from their marketing department.

Raise your expectations of what marketing can provide and step back to look at your services sales cycle from a marketing perspective.

> 🕮 **For a services organization, your marketing focus kicks in once the product sale is closed.**

Think of the service sales cycle as a clock divided into 4 quadrants:

- Noon – 3:00pm (building awareness and generating leads)
- 3-6pm (advancing the opportunity and closing the sale)
- 6-9pm (services delivery, customer satisfaction)
- 9pm-Midnight (up-sell/cross-sell)

In a product sales cycle, 100% of your marketing budget is normally directed at Noon – 6:00pm. But for a services organization, your focus kicks in once the product sale is closed. What marketing materials do you need for that period? What do you need for following up and generating more business? What do you need to help sales close the business with services included?

To help close the sale, marketing should work closely with sales to provide customer discussion documents (questions to ask or key points to listen for to know what services would be appropriate for the customer), provide content for proposals and have customer success stories or references available. Other than those limited items, a service organization should ask marketing for help in the 6:00pm-Midnight section. Marketing should be asking the service organization to generate content that can be used for magazine articles and white papers and arrange for key members of the service organization to speak at conferences and events. Those two activities will do more to build credibility for your service organization than having a datasheet and PowerPoint on all your services.

Once services are sold, marketing can provide two key areas of assistance. If the service to be provided will be disruptive to the customer's clients, marketing can support the customer's IT group by explaining benefits of the changes to the overall organization. IT rarely has marketing dollars so this service is normally welcomed as a true value-add. Marketing should also provide assistance in measuring customer satisfaction/loyalty as the service is delivered and completed. Both activities will give the marketing team the information they need to evaluate what services were purchased and why they were purchased. More marketing focus on the value of the services to the customer will yield more relevant services packages and services positioning in the future.

Finally, by involving marketing in the crucial delivery period, they will learn how to cross-sell and up-sell which is vitally important to every organization and where marketing normally plays a limited role.

Kathy Macchi, Principal, Allegro Associates

90 You – The Candidate

If you work in marketing professional services—or in delivering professional services—you would do well to take a page from your local politician's campaign playbook. Sure, it's easy to make fun of politicians and the political system (OK, it is really easy!) but keep in mind that survey after survey reveals that while voters might not like the general state of politics or politicians, in general, they sure like their local government official. As one pundit quipped, "the voters seem to say they don't like those guys, but they do love their guy," or gal as the case may be. Good consultants can easily imagine their clients saying to them, "Gee, I don't like consultants, but I am sure glad I have you working on this project."

The reality is that marketing or delivering professional services is rarely black and white. It's all about power, sure, but it's also about messaging, compromise, teaming, communicating—and delivering. And, what better model to look to for advice than the political arena where messages, teaming, communicating and delivering are all tested in what can only be described as a harsh environment.

So what is the lesson? There are three.

First, in addition to being a consultant, you are a candidate. You have a message to deliver, you have to work with people to do it, you have to deliver value and you have to demonstrate exactly how you delivered that value. And, you are always on. You the candidate will be tested round the clock and in every interaction. I used to know a terrifically skilled guy—a real honest to goodness sales genius—who believed it was all about results. He never understood it was about the politics of results, too. He lost his job. The new guy who replaced him? She might as well have been running for the Senate. She delivered value—and she adeptly proved she delivered value!

Second, the client is the voter. Sometimes we forget but the client does have a vote. The services market is incredibly competitive. Your clients do have a choice and whether you like it or not they have a choice to vote you into their business, their project and their budget—or not. Take a moment to think about your current client base. Go ahead, step off the campaign trail for a minute, grab a cup of coffee, put the Blackberry down and step away from the monitor. Turn your cell phone off. Now, think about the last half dozen interactions you have had with your client. Now ask yourself one question about those most recent conversations. Do you think a political candidate running for re-election would have talked to a prospective voter the way you did? You are the candidate, clients are voters and they do have a choice.

Politics is the new best practice. It's also about messaging, compromise, teaming, communicating – and delivering.

Finally, every time you interact with your client you are in the middle of an election—a fight for your very political life! Want to know how local politicians really survive? Between their election cycles they interact with their constituents. They listen to them. They deliver on funding for a playground, they attend the local High School's concert and they

visit with local shopkeepers. In short, they use every interaction they have with their constituents to prove they deserve their position—and to be re-elected. Of course, I am not suggesting that you only live in re-election mode. That's shallow and sooner or later your client will find you out. Yet, take a look at your current client (or your most prominent client or clients). Are you delivering value and demonstrating value to that client during the current contract and before it is up for renewal? If not, you might do well to take a page from the playbook of your local elected representative—you are a candidate, your client is a voter and if you want to win and retain the business, you might do well to strive for re-election in every interaction you have.
(Note: This tip reflects the personal views of the author and not the official opinion or policy of IBM).

JP Frenza, eBassador, IBM

91 A Picture Says a Thousand Words

"A picture says a thousand words" - an over-used adage which is also often ignored. Generally, when you are trying to convey an important message to an extremely busy client (Sales proposal, key risk, key issue, etc.), they often make a decision on whether it is important within the first 3 minutes.

Too many times, consultants prepare reams of data, large excel sheets, 100 page PowerPoint decks, etc. and the size alone turns off the audience before a word is said. It is worth investing time to learn the graphic capabilities of PowerPoint, word and excel along with an understanding of the type of pictures which will hit a chord with the audience. Selecting the appropriate metaphors, graphics and colors will make a huge improvement in the reception of the message being conveyed.

Keep graphics simple and appropriate.

In summary: Keep graphics simple and appropriate

Be aware of your client's list of corporate or personal picture/color/format aversions e.g., one well-known cola company uses red, the other uses blue.

Learn to use the correct types of graphs and metaphors - it's amazing to see how many people just pick the first format.

Ian Plows, Delivery/Midwest Technology Strategy, Architecture & Design, Capgemini

92 Know Your Audience

I don't know how many times I have seen proposals or presentations that are focused on the vendor rather than the customer.

If you start out by singing the praises of your product or service you are very likely to have your audience turn off and be lost to you, not only for the presentation or proposal but also for the sale. The term 'product vomit' describes this phenomenon quite graphically and quite well. Keep that picture in mind when you are presenting or proposing and you'll be far less likely to make your potential customer sick.

> **Stay focused on the solution and its value and only talk about the things you bring to the table that are relevant to the solution and to value.**

Other than starting with 'ABC Software is pleased to present XYZ customer with ...' your company and its products and services should not be mentioned until you have made sure that you've done two things. One, establish who your customer is and what their business is. Two, describe and discuss the reason that the customer is talking to you, i.e., the problem or opportunity that the customer wants addressed. Only then is it appropriate to say: 'ABC Software can provide a solution to XYZ's ..." and go on to explain that solution and why it is a good one. Stay focused on the solution and its value and only talk about the things you bring to the table that are relevant to the solution and to value. Include case studies and references that speak to the solution and to value. Relegate product details, background information, execution details, even pricing, and the like to the end or to appendices and glossy brochures.

In short, make sure your audience knows that you know who you are speaking to and knows that you have listened to them and understand them -- their business as well as their problem or opportunity. Then tell them directly about, and only about, what you have that addresses their issues. Give evidence that you've done it before. The rest should be footnotes.

Alvin Begun, President, Begun Consulting

93 Craftsmanship or Production?

Professional services teams are excellent at "making the trains move on time." They focus on customer relationships and meeting deliverables by closely tracking operating metrics. However, surprisingly, even some of the largest professional services organizations lack the organizational precedence of "productizing" services or investing in packaging today in order to maximize their operations downstream.

Services teams have "best practices" and re-use workflows and business processes from prior "engagements," but such repurposing is often tactical, not formally productized, rarely "product managed" and certainly not marketed. Delivery costs create pressure to maximize deal-by-deal margin and short-term operating performance. As a result, professional services groups, particularly those within software companies, often succeed by becoming excellent craftsmen, but terrible manufacturers of solutions.

Use the leverage of productization of Professional Services to deliver a triple-win to the customer, your company and your PSO.

The norm in the software business is to invest ten or fifteen percent of revenues into R&D - forever - in order to create and continually improve the re-usable intellectual property called software. But professional services teams tend not to budget in this way and do not have such an expectation, even though the difference between a 25 percent and 40 percent project margin can often be directly linked to the amount of leverage a team has created from their past investments.

Thankfully there are many ways to create leverage. Process leverage standardizes on best practices, engagement models and workflows. Technology leverage creates advantage through standardizing on automation tools, core technologies and reusable intellectual property. Product leverage repurposes standard product components. Of course, the leverage value goes way up as each type of leverage gets created and then augmented as a result of each engagement.

The last kind of leverage is application or solution leverage. This occurs when, as a result of experience gained solving specific problems, the organization leverages all of their other intellectual property, products, processes and tools. As a result, they predict with a level of confidence what the solution implementation will cost early on in the selling cycle and they replicate it with high confidence. When this occurs, applications or solutions can then be "productized," and a sale can be priced based on value to the client rather than based on cost. In this situation, everyone wins. The customer wins because of better predictability and quality as well as reduced implementation time and cost. The service team wins too because by pricing based on business value rather than cost, they can generally extract higher margins than what they would otherwise have been able to achieve.

Michael Tanner, Managing Director, Adexta Inc.

94 Enterprise Applications Packages Offerings

Most organizations find implementing an ERP application a daunting task, especially in the mid-market. At KPMG Consulting, before it became BearingPoint, we developed a series of offerings called R2i – Rapid Return on Investment, initially around Oracle ERP. We had a pre-configured Oracle Application solution that we could get up and running in a SMB company within a few months.

> **Utilizing the inherent capabilities of the enterprise application allows faster implementations with an easier upgrade path.**

We had a lab environment to host a customer's project (one of the selling points) and then image copy their system over to their own hardware once they got it in place. This also provided an easy way to re-sell hardware which we made a nice margin on too.

The offerings were far better than a generic methodology which everyone has. They were better than a targeted methodology with tools that some people have. The offerings took it a step further as we had real, working, configured applications that we could show prospects in the sales process.

From a delivery perspective, instead of starting with a clean sheet of paper, we started with a working solution. Instead of asking, "How do you want to do this function or business process?" we stated "this is how this function or business process works best with this application and this is a standard industry practice". If the prospect said that they wanted to do it a different way, instead of the typical consulting answer, we asked why? We explained that the only really good reason to deviate from the standard practice was to gain competitive or business advantage by doing it a different way, not because it is the way they used to do it.

Even though this was targeted towards the mid-market, it was also a great entrée into large organizations. Especially those who wanted to do a phased implementation by business unit or geography. Getting quick wins helps secure funding and organizational buy-in for subsequent phases and builds credibility and improves your referenceability.

Utilizing the inherent capabilities of the enterprise application allows faster implementations with an easier upgrade path. The more you customize, the more likely you will need to re-implement rather than upgrade. Imitation being the sincerest form of flattery, Oracle developed a similar set of offerings called Fast Forward and so did many others.

Michael Resnick

95 How to Make Services Offers Stick

We were having challenges getting our consultants to use the artifacts that had been built over many years in the field. We had created service offerings in the past, but there was a negative perception about their value. We did a survey with people in the field and found that most consultants had not actually looked at what was available, mainly for two reasons:

- The content was too hard to find
- The consultants weren't measured on using or contributing to the artifact library, and received no real recognition for doing so

Here are the main areas we considered and took action on:

Ensure that the content is good or cut it - we chose the top consultants in the field to validate the content and fix it. We signed their names to the offering, so they felt responsible for it, and were measured on the success of it.

> 📖 **Use the same rigor and discipline in creating and maintaining your service offerings as you do for your products.**

Be picky. If an offering wasn't of high enough quality, we wouldn't release it. We were rigorous about the quality, and wanted to set the bar high so people in the field would learn that if it's a published offering, it must be good.

Put someone in charge of ensuring consistency between the offerings. Every offering must have the same look and feel, and each must go through the same process (enablement, validation, sign off) or the quality will suffer.

Make it easy to find the content - we reorganized our portal so that it was easy for consultants to browse and find the content they were looking for, and tested it with new hires.

We used our own governance product that we modified for our PS needs. This product first captured a booked order of a service offering, then opened a project similar to MS project, and then coupled the service offering assets to this project so it would be easy for a consultant to use.

Invest in training and enablement - we conducted internet training for our consultants in the field. One hour long sessions on what's out there, how to find it, and why it's good for them and their customers. And don't forget to train your managers, they are the ones to help enforce usage, and if they aren't bought in, you may as well forget it.

We trained the software sales force, who got compensated for selling services. Getting their buy-in was key because it put even more pressure on our own organization to sell our Service Packages. Offerings make it easy for salespeople to justify to customers what they are buying, so they are generally in favor.

Find ways to enforce (or encourage) usage - we set up quick and easy 5 question surveys about the offering that each consultant filled out after using it.

We wrote a quarterly newsletter and included quotes from consultants and salespeople who gave kudos about the success of the offerings. We created a culture of thanking everyone who contributed to content creation and reviews.

We added MBOs to consultant's bonus plans to use and add to content.

Measure the cost/value of the service offerings - service offerings can be an expensive proposition, so it is critical to ensure that the value you get from them is high. A business case was built before we created an offering, and then we measured how much revenue it brought in, as well as customer satisfaction and consultant usage satisfaction. At a certain point in time, we needed to kill an offering when the maintenance cost outweighed its benefit.

Dione Hedgpeth

96 Demand Generation

Demand generation for a services organization in a product company needs to address two audiences: internal and external. For any professional services organization starting up, internal marketing is key to jumpstarting your business. If your sales force is not sold on your ability to deliver services and can't articulate the value services provide, no services will be sold.

I've seen many internally focused programs but the best have included:

"Fun" kick-off style event to announce the program.

Five or six PowerPoint slides that a sales representative can incorporate into his current product pitch.

📖 **For any professional services organization starting up, internal marketing is key to jumpstarting your business.**

A positioning document stating in one paragraph what the services group does, why it is unique, and why it matters, with a list of the service organization capabilities, benefits and proof points.

White papers authored by people in the services organization.

A sales-friendly process for engaging the services organization.

Audio tapes of sales reps with positive customer stories to tell about the value services brought to their customer.

The PowerPoint slides and positioning documents are the basic marketing materials required to launch services but the other items are what you'll need to sell your services.

White papers are the pieces that build the credibility of the service organization in the minds of the sales staff. A sales-friendly engagement process shows the service organization wants to work with sales and is not operating for its own benefit. However, to really win over your sales staff, they need to hear from their own that engaging the service organization is to their benefit. Marketing-driven success stories won't do that. No one believes them, but sales people believe other sales people. Have that full combination of materials and you're on your way to building demand for your services.

Kathy Macchi, Principal, Allegro Associates

97 Lead Generation That Works

The path to revenue for service providers is three-pronged: winning the client, successfully completing the project, and retaining the client. No matter what particular area of consulting you are engaged in, the cycle is the same. The key to keeping all company resources working and revenue flowing is to have a steady pipeline of clients.

Today's dilemma is that many businesses lack a corporate-wide strategy for winning new clients, relying on rather haphazard measures to learn about new business opportunities and locate areas for new first-time business. Whether the means of reaching new prospects is through print ads, the Internet, cold calling on the telephone, references, or multi-faceted campaigns, all service providers need to have a consolidated way to locate, target and build their client base, and have the metrics to evaluate which marketing means were actually best tied to successful client acquisition. Knowing what means of reaching a new lead best correlate with the advancement to a prospect and to a client under contract not only optimizes the ROI from a company's allocated marketing dollars, but also decreases the time to contract award, and lowers the total client attainment costs through focusing only on programs that actually yield new clients.

> **Key to keeping all company resources working and revenue flowing is to have a steady pipeline of clients.**

Maximizing visibility can best be accommodated electronically -- by keeping track of the sources of leads and by campaign management that targets, locates and builds the client base desired. Use of keywords in web campaigns and the necessary on-line lead capture of the ensuing leads are pivotal in successful lead management. Simple forms can help you capture a lead from visitors at your web site, from your webinars (you can create forms in WebEx, for example), or from downloadable white papers.

The key questions include:

- Where do most of my leads come from?
- Where do leads come from that turn out to be my best clients? (and which are the worst?)
- Where do leads come from that lead to the highest-paying projects?
- Where do leads come from that lead to the clients that are retained the longest? These are those clients who are more than "satisfied" – they are loyal.

Then measure these against the cost of attaining the lead through that particular source. This is an area consultants rarely spend time to think about. How many conversations did you require (your time is billable), how many speeches did you give or how many conferences did you attend to get that business?

With the goal, then, of accelerating the conversion of leads to actual contracts, what processes and procedures need to be integrated for success? After all, there are multiple parties involved: the Marketing VP responsible for building the lead chain; the Sales Representative who works the opportunity and ultimately closes the deal; and the Project Manager who has to accurately scope the engagement for the proposal and the contract. Here you need to ascertain the cost to move the client from prospect to client, and the length of the sales cycle. The goal: getting that cycle shorter with the least amount of human effort in the process.

Meanwhile, the business requirement is for an integrated view of the prospect, allowing each involved party visibility into the same information in real-time, so the data one reviews is never out of date – and each person sees exactly the same data – all the time. This is where software solutions can come into play – but no amount of software will compensate for a sloppy strategy!

Dr. Katherine Jones, Director of Marketing, NetSuite Inc.

98 Customer Satisfaction Tools

Creating loyal, referenceable customers is one of the most important elements for any company's future success. Making every client "wildly satisfied" should be a top priority. Client satisfaction is based on setting proper expectations during the sales, proposal and contract process and delivering high-quality solutions that meet or exceed those expectations.

> Customer satisfaction and referenceability must be primary goals for all employees.

Do what you say you will do and always let your client know what to expect - how the project will be conducted, the roles of the project team, timelines, deliverables and escalation path. Clear and open communication – for good and bad news – is essential. Another key ingredient is to ensure proper handoffs from all customer-facing personnel. Finally, customer satisfaction and referenceability must be a primary goal for all employees so it is important to consistently and effectively measure customer satisfaction and make it an essential part of all client engagements and employee measurements.

There are a plethora of excellent customer and employee satisfaction survey tools, most are web-based, easy to use and provide excellent reporting and analytics. However, I have found that the best way to improve customer satisfaction is to not measure it after-the-fact in a survey but to proactively promote client delight through direct, personal interactions with your customers.

Post-engagement Satisfaction Survey - A direct, in-person or over the phone engagement satisfaction survey should be conducted at the end of every project. The Project Management Office is probably the best group to conduct the survey but it could also be conducted by Sales or Marketing. The survey should be short and simple with the key question "Would you recommend us?" Make sure the results are reviewed and discussed during your weekly executive team meeting. Make sure you immediately respond to issues surfaced in the survey.

Publish "Go Lives" for every project - "Go Lives" should be published internally for all projects to communicate the business value of the solution and as a first step in creating customer testimonials. Completing the "Go-Live" template should be a mandatory part of your project close-out process.

Customer Video Tapes – Have the project team conduct an in-person video interview with your referenceable client executive sponsors. The videos can be used in future customer presentations or emailed to prospects to minimize "overusing" your client references. These videos are also an excellent training tool for new employees to showcase the value of your solutions.

Client Executive Sponsors - Create a named "Client Executive" – a member of the Executive team - who will maintain an executive client relationship and act as the client sponsor and escalation point. A good way to start the Executive relationship is for the named client executive to send a brief introductory letter to let the client know he/she takes Customer Satisfaction seriously and is interested in their candid feedback. Follow-up with an in-person or telephone meeting.

Customer Advisory Board – create a Customer Advisory Board comprised of your top clients – two Customer delegates – the most senior IT and Business executives – no substitutions. Set up an annual Customer Advisory Board meeting to review your company's strategy and progress, showcase new solutions, hold discussions around topical subjects and have Customer's present best practices and lessons learned. If properly managed, your Customer Advisory Board will become your best advocates and provide valuable feedback and guidance for your strategy and solutions.

Jeanne Urich, Management Consultant, Adexta

99 Marketing Improves Project Success

In web-based software project implementations what customers think they want and what meets their business requirements are at times worlds apart. Narrowing this gap is essential to completing a successful project. The ways I have found success in doing this are:

Work with marketing to create one page service overviews. Have your resource teams clearly define what they can deliver with estimated delivery times. These can be used by the sales team to correctly set expectations up-front.

PS controls scoping and estimating. When the sales team finds a customer ready to scope a project, have an experienced implementer work directly with the customer to create the scope of work. If there is not time to complete a detailed SOW prior to signing the contract, include text in the contract stating a detailed SOW will be delivered within a finite timeframe.

Work with marketing to create one page overviews. Have your resource teams clearly define what they can deliver with estimated delivery times.

Always include what is out of scope. Usually during the sales process there are items that come up that a client really wants but cannot have at this time for budgetary or other reasons. State these in the SOW. This can pay huge dividends when trying to avoid scope creep.

During implementation don't let issues linger. If there are items that you know you cannot deliver tell the customer immediately. A seemingly small issue can snowball over time into a large "I just thought you could do that" or "I was never told I could not do that" which may require extraordinary effort to get back to where you would have been had you just said no up-front.

Manage a project to a plan. This seems simple but more often than not an initial project plan goes for long periods without being updated, leading the project to be off track.

Clear and regular communication and documentation. Have a communication plan and follow it. This should also include an escalation plan for both your clients and your organization. Document status on a regular basis and publish to a central location.

"Own" the project. Ensure your project teams strive for a full understanding of the project goals and success criteria. Put yourself in the customer's shoes during implementation and anticipate their needs.

In most cases, you are the expert and the customer looks to you for guidance. For example, if there is a "Contact us" section ask the customer if you can send a copy to your email so you can monitor and fix any technical issues.

John Murphy, VP, Professional Services, Kintera Inc.

100 Customer Satisfaction Survey

Our Marketing department hired an outside firm to run a customer-sat survey. Without involving our services team or account execs, the firm promptly approached a number of customers with a set of canned questions. Since this was a marketing initiative, the questions were biased towards finding new opportunities, rather than seriously gauging customer-sat. Although a majority of customers reported being satisfied with the product, a minority raised issues. The marketing firm could only take notes and report back to HQ. This caused a storm within the management team, leading to multiple conference calls with each of the customers. This time, the services team and account execs were involved to address the customer's issues. We overcame the mini-crisis, but what started out as a positive, pro-active initiative on our side ended up as a knee-jerk reaction. Moral of the story: hold customer-sat surveys regularly, but have your account manager(s) or a services exec participate on the calls to take ownership of any issues that may arise.

Anonymous

6. Services Selling

This chapter covers topics such as how to work with product sales, service sales compensation, negotiating, pricing and closing the deal.

"I take time to lick the customer's face, I wag my tail when they talk, I jump up and down when they walk through the door. That's what sets me apart from all the other sales people!"

101 When Y'all Say 'Constituents' .... Do Y'all Mean 'Folks'?

On an engagement for a worldwide express company, a small boutique consulting partner asked us to attend the presentation of their software solution that used our products to manage the client's marketing budgets and marketing campaigns.

One by one the room filled with representatives from several organizations across the company until each vacant seat, and even our own comfy armchairs, were occupied by employees of the freight forwarder, all anxious to hear how we would enable them to contain their marketing costs and optimize their budget.

📖 **Know your audience and familiarize yourself with their industry vernacular.**

The partner had an opportunity to fan their tail feathers and dazzle a captive audience with an arsenal of 10 cent technology concepts like "conversion rate", "JavaScript", "cost per click" and "burstable bandwidth" and they referred to the users throughout as "constituents". It really was a nice presentation. It wasn't until the Q&A slide when I saw a hand raised sheepishly in the back of the room.

The question asked <Southern accent for effect>: "When y'all say 'constituents' .... do y'all mean 'folks'?"

To this day, I don't know if any of the other terms even registered with the audience, but I'll never forget the lesson learned there. The presentation was clearly written for a different audience. This was a functional audience interested in hearing how the software was going to improve their day and make them more productive. They weren't particularly interested in the technical aspects of how we would achieve this. I reflect on this often and it reminds me how important it is to understand the customer. It never hurts to take notice of the stuff on their desks, the pictures that adorn their offices and workspace. Pay attention to those things that make them unique with history, interests, life experiences, families and lives outside of work. Be humble and gracious and know your audience. Keep in mind that technical solutions often result in a reduction in force of very hardworking and committed employees. Tailor your message appropriately.

Anonymous

102 Consultantitis

The consultant's role is to be informed, have mastery and expertise in a subject area and have a disposition to help and support clients. No one could argue with these qualities – except perhaps in a pre-sales situation! As a professional services sales executive, I have seen time and again how "the consultant's gene" – the drive to show competence and a willingness to solve issues – can upset a sales cycle. Sometimes it is the innocent desire to solve a problem (even before a problem is actually identified) or the drive to appear the most knowledgeable in the room. The DNA that makes a consultant an asset during project rollout can stop a sales cycle in its tracks.

> 🕮 **The DNA that makes a consultant an asset during project rollout can stop a sales cycle in its tracks.**

Let me give you an example. Some years ago, we were pitching our ERP strategy to a large multi-national corporation; it was a significant software and services deal. The client was down to two vendors: us and another ERP player. Our "coach" on the client's selection team had told us that we were in a lead position; but it was far from a done deal since one or two members of the selection committee were pulling for the competition.

In the final round of presentations, things were going well. The ERP system was demonstrating beautifully and our consultants were knowledgeable and crisp in their replies to the client's questions. We had a good chance of winning this. We had just finished an explanation of how we would implement the manufacturing module and had walked through the workstation processes when a question came from the audience. It was an innocent question that should have caused us no problem, but it killed the deal.

"Does your work station program run against a calendar?" asked one of the members of the selection team. The answer was "yes", and if the answer "yes" had been given we would have probably won the deal.

"Yes!" said our manufacturing consultant, "it does, it runs against a 52-week calendar." At this point, we were still in the lead. But the consultant wanted to bedazzle the crowd with his expertise. "Now," he continued "...if you're running a 53-week calendar it's a bit tricky, let me explain a great work around for you," and off he went.

"What?" said one of the selection committee, "you don't have the facility to run a 53-week calendar? We need a 53-week calendar!" All of a sudden, the need for a 53-week calendar became a huge issue. An issue that had not existed just minutes earlier. For the next 45 minutes a heated discussion erupted amongst the selection committee. It became impossible for us to move the discussion forward. We never completed our presentation.

The following day the selection committee met with our competitors. The competition had been prepped on the calendar issue in advance of their presentation – they too had a "coach". As it happens, the competitor's software only had a 52-week production calendar too, but they were primed and prepared for the "calendar" question. They answered the question quickly and went on to complete their presentation. Needless to say, they ended up winning the business.

In our win/loss analysis, we referred to this as the "53-week calendar deal". Calendaring the workstations was never an issue for the client until we made it one. We were told that we lost the deal on this issue alone. I clearly recall that "Win/Loss report" - under the heading "Reason for Loss" the word "Consultantitis" was written.

Dave Brown, IBM Alliance Leader, Capgemini

103 Actively Listen to Your Customer Before You Respond

Many consultants seem overly anxious to answer a client's question, but before they've really heard (and understood) it.

Remember that clients are people, and people want to be heard. Many times, I observe consultants demonstrating that they haven't understood what a client has said yet they give an answer anyway. This problem is exacerbated when working with global teams made up of people whose first language is something other than English (more on this momentarily).

In frequent coaching sessions with consultants on this topic, I often advise them to practice active listening skills, and then carefully consider the appropriate answer before actually delivering it. To put this in "actionable" terms, I encourage them to frequently paraphrase what the client has said before getting to the answer. One benefit of this is that it gives the consultant the chance to consider his/her answer while "restating" the client's question. If it takes a few moments of silence for the consultant to formulate their answer, this is fine - and it is better than answering a question that the client has not asked.

> 📖 **Invest a few minutes to really understand what the customer is saying.**

Experience has proven that paraphrasing and patience are even more important when working with non-native English speakers. Keep in mind that they are integral members of the team (and again, they want to be heard, and they want to contribute), and are not speaking in their native language. Investing a few minutes to really understand their point is almost always worthwhile.

These techniques have repeatedly helped me succeed in establishing rapport with both team members and clients. This rapport has led to trust, and the trust has resulted in high performing teams and satisfied clients. Satisfied clients often buy additional services.

Steven Mollen, Sirius Solutions

104 Never Assume

I recently was engaged in selling a CRM project to a prospect where our champion, we were told, was fresh from an SAP implementation and in fact had built his reputation from the SAP project. The prospect had also used SAP consultants for the roll-out. The prospect is a $1B plus organization with 550 sales reps stretched across 3 business units. I'm envisioning a potential six-figure deal. We presented our offerings and performed the scoping sessions, which went very well with excellent participation and feedback. At the end of the scoping session, our champion comes forward and states, "Your sales representative told me that it will cost about $30K to implement, so that is all I have asked for in my budget."

📖 **Just because a prospect carries the 'big project' label do not assume he has run a similar project.**

It turns out our "champion" had arrived late on the SAP project. He had no experience with software vendors and their associated Professional Services. Our champion focused on rates and went with third party consultants based on lowest perceived cost. Our sales representative was severely reprimanded for mismanaging expectations.

Michael J. Lopez, Practice Director, SalesForce.com

105 Building a Repeatable Process to Support Sales

Despite the complex solutions that many consulting organizations pitch, they fail to build a team and a repeatable process to support sales. It's ironic when you consider the sophisticated sales engineering organizations that exist to support most complicated technical product sales cycles. Instead, consulting organizations typically operate in a reactive mode and rely on "who is available" to support sales. Unfortunately this approach often results in deployment of resources that don't have the product, solution or selling skills necessary to close a big deal. After learning this lesson the hard way, I took a different, more proactive approach to sales support by building a dedicated, rotationally staffed team to address the unique dynamics of selling services. In planning for the implementation of this

📖 **Consulting organizations typically operate in a reactive mode and rely on "who is available" to support sales.**

team, I diligently tracked business development hours for one quarter to ensure that I "right sized" the team. Additionally, I paid particular attention to historical sales trends as well as future forecasts to ensure that the resources on the team adequately reflected the solutions we were selling. After implementing this approach, we saw the following benefits:

We were able to reduce total hours spent on business development as a whole because we had a critical mass of resources doing nothing but business development support and they became very effective at the tasks common to every sales pursuit (RFP responses, estimating, presentation preparation, etc.). Essentially we built a knowledge base of re-useable sales collateral and stopped reinventing the wheel on every sales pursuit.

We increased "customer satisfaction" within the product and consulting sales teams as our responsiveness, quality, and ability to help close product deals improved. We were no longer "confusing sales with delivery". We were selling good business and driving better close rates.

Employee morale increased, as we were no longer asking resources staffed full-time at a customer site to help with business development after hours and on weekends. Additionally, a rotation through the business development team was an opportunity for a road warrior to get off the road for a period of time (or at least typically not travel Monday through Friday to a customer site), recharge, and focus on a diverse set of accounts and challenges.

Jason Blessing, General Manager, Taleo Business Edition

106 Helping Project Sponsors Get Buy-in

One of the challenges of a new application deployment is getting a company's members excited about the deployment. This was the situation when the executives of a large multi-national company were in the process of deciding to purchase our supply chain application. They had the daunting task of generating excitement throughout the various operations in several different countries within Asia.

To address this issue for the sponsor we provided a planning workshop that we expanded to include team building and a project strategy workshop.

We brought in the operations managers from various countries and held a three-day workshop to review strategy for the project (who, how, when and what). In addition, we helped the teams to build trust and relationships through group activities interspersed during the 3 days. As we gained agreement on the strategy and schedules for the project, we prepared a strategy document that described the conclusions of the team. This document was signed by the operations managers from each of the countries represented. We provided this document to the sponsor to clearly show that his team was behind him on the project.

> 🕮 **A well-defined workshop can build good team spirit and inspire confidence in project success.**

The multi-million dollar deal was signed within a couple of days after the completion of the workshop.

Peter Wong, Manager, Nextance Inc.

107 How to Improve Your Sales Win Rate

We found ourselves in a situation where we were going after more deals than our team could complete with a high degree of quality. We did some analysis and saw that we were losing some deals we shouldn't mainly because of quality and/or execution issues. Additionally, we had a number of deals where the prospect didn't go forward with the project at all due to budget, lack of sponsorship, competing initiatives, or other customer-specific issues.

We had to focus on two issues – improve our win rate and stop chasing bad deals. Both of these issues were the result of poor or no qualification. We were too quick to jump on a deal instead of spending the proper amount of time making sure the

> 🕮 **The deal qualification process resulted in a higher success rate on the deals we pursued, and we won deals we would have historically lost.**

customer had the budget and approval to proceed with the project. We needed to make sure we were interfacing with the decision makers and weren't being used as a negotiation tactic for another firm who had the inside track. The result of chasing every deal was that we weren't properly focusing our efforts on the good deals that we should win or at least had a good shot of winning. Spending cycles on non-qualified deals was reducing the time, quality, and management attention we should have been focusing on fewer, but more qualified deals.

We put together a Deal Qualification process that included the consulting sales, delivery, and management teams. The consulting sales team sometimes didn't like the process, but it quickly showed which deals were qualified and which ones were not. Not surprisingly, the better sales people brought quality, qualified deals to the Deal Qualification meetings, and we agreed to focus our efforts on pursuing and winning those deals. Alternatively, we would quickly decide not to pursue a deal if it wasn't properly qualified, either as a real deal or one that we had very little chance to win for whatever reason.

The result of the Deal Qualification process was not only a higher success rate on the deals we pursued, but also winning some deals we would have historically lost. This was because we had a better focus from a time and level of effort, quality, and management support perspective. We had a laser approach, not a shotgun!

Derek Wolf, VP, Services Sales, Taleo

108 Selling Services for a Partner-Centric Software Company

The challenge that most Professional Services sales professionals face is dealing with the System Integrators (SIs) that their companies use to drive software license sales.

Having sat on the PS side of the fence I have learned that the wrong approach is to try and compete head to head with the SI partner. The SI has the upper hand in most cases because they are in the deal earlier. If they perceive you as a threat they will implement measures to insure you never get an invitation to the party.

To compound the issue, the biggest sponsor of the SI is the internal software sales representative that sees them as someone that is 1) creating additional sales pipeline; 2) perceived as easier to work with; 3) typically can "invest" in the sales cycle; and 4) reduces the company's and the sales rep's risk by eliminating revenue recognition and other challenges. Even if your company compensates the software reps for services sales they still will not always include you in the process. The reality is their first and last priority is to get the license deal sooner rather than later and at the maximum dollar value. They keep their jobs and go to club if they hit their software number!

Take a multiple-channel approach by selling to the software sales rep, the prospect and the system integrator.

Additionally, the prospect has typically been working with the SI for an extended period of time and in some cases even before the software sales representative was introduced into the account. They have "invested" in the customer and the customer believes that the SI understands their business and challenges. If even invited to the process, the PS organization is brought in later and can be perceived as an outsider.

The key to successful selling in this type of environment is to first understand the aforementioned challenges and take what I like to call a multiple-channel approach to selling into 1) the software sales rep; 2) the prospect; and 3) the System Integrator.

With the internal software sales rep you need to "make it personal". A relationship with the rep is critical to your success in being invited to the process early and often. You need to make them feel comfortable that 1) you will not elongate the deal cycle; 2) not create any revenue recognition issues so they will get paid; 3) make them feel comfortable that you will work with the SI partner and not contradict the partner in front of the prospect; and 4) you can provide value to their process. If you get engaged earlier and add value then you will gain the recognition and trust of the sales rep and the prospect. You will also create a level playing field for you with the SI as the customer will value your input to help them solve their business challenges. In certain cases you will not get the opportunity to sell services but you should engage for the benefit of your relationship with the rep, partner and customer anyway.

On the prospect front, assuming you can get in early, the key is to insure they understand your value proposition and how PS complements the SI. In some cases prospects do not recognize the value of having their software provider involved in their implementation efforts. It is key to show you not only know your product but you also understand the prospect's industry. Research the company and industry and make sure you find the opportunity to share your knowledge with the prospect. I have seen deals won or lost due to the industry knowledge (actual or perceived) of the service provider.

The toughest nut of this triad is the System Integrator partner! They typically have the upper hand with their ties to the sales rep and are engaged earlier with the prospect. The key here, like with the sales rep, is to build a personal relationship with the partner. This can be challenging since there are many key personnel that you need to deal with but it will be well worth your time. Also, if you have an internal alliance/partner manager, work with them to help with the partner relationship. Like the sales rep, you must convince them that you are not a threat to their revenue stream and you can add value. If they see that you have won the hearts and minds of the sales rep and the prospect and you can "complement" their offering they will work with you.

You need to be proactive. If you wait for a deal to come to you without first building relationships with your internal license sales organization and the SI partner there is a high probability you will not succeed.

Douglas H. Moore, Professional Services,
Sales Management Executive

109 SaaS - Sell and Deliver What You Have

The "old" model, license-on-customer-premises software world gave Sales, Pre-Sales, and Professional Services a lot of leeway in tailoring a solution to fit the customer's needs. Depending on the product and level of configurability, we were free to shape the solution to desired business processes, create new and innovative integrations to external systems, creatively mix and match functions to address a new vertical, and at times tweak things to such a degree that the end implementation looked nothing like what Product Management had originally envisioned.

Within the Software-as-a-Service (SaaS) world, there is often a high degree of configurability, but much more care must be taken in selling and delivering a solution that conforms to the current product.

> **In a SaaS model, more care must be taken in selling and delivering a solution that conforms to the current product.**

Changes that might be inconsequential in the old model, such as modifying a field length, creating an interface to an external system, or adding support for a new data object, may, depending on the SaaS product, require a new release from your Product organization.

When push comes to shove and the pressure to close a sale increases, Sales concessions are often made for items outside current product capabilities. And if your PS team doesn't understand what is in your product, they may agree to non-conforming requirements during the project. Add enough of these up and you can quickly create a situation that impacts multiple customers as releases are thrown off, resources are reallocated, and quality decreases due to crashed schedules.

So, the tip is, sell and deliver what is in the product today. Even if you sell what is expected to be in a future release in time for a customer go-live, you are running the risk that release schedules may slip. The pressure to violate this tip will be intense as startups struggle to achieve the life blood of new revenue. If you choose to violate this, make sure all groups are on board and accountable. To be successful in SaaS, Product organizations must also show leadership in defining and defending the release schedule. In my experience a reactive, "customer knows best" approach to product requirements is very hard to make successful in a Software-as-a-Service play.

Gary Schaumburg, Services Advantage

110 SaaS - Don't Sell Your Projects Short

Everybody talks about "ease of implementation" being one of the key benefits of the SaaS model. And there is a lot of truth to this. The tighter solutions usually provided by SaaS, the fact that hardware and software do not need to be installed on the customer premises, and the lack of associated technical training and administration associated with an "on-premises" installation are some of the savings that the SaaS model provides.

However, this premise is often taken by clients, sales people, and PS managers new to the SaaS arena to mean that such activities as client-side project management, business process redesign, change management, best practices consulting, and user training will also be much "lighter" in a SaaS model. My experience has been that this is not the case. You will need to exert at least the same level of project management and control that you would in the old model. In fact, you may need to bring an even higher level of project rigor since a SaaS solution may require the client's organization to adapt to your solution to a larger degree than in the old model. For instance, the SaaS solution may require client processes to be modified to fit your product if your configurability is somewhat less than that found in a competing on-premises package. Change management to adopt the new solution within the client organization is really no less than in the old model. And end-user training on the new solution can be a very large task, depending on the size of the departments affected by the new tool.

> You need to bring an even higher level of project rigor to a SaaS solution.

So, you probably know what you need to do for each of these activities. They'll be very similar to what you would have done in an old model implementation. The challenge is to fight the perception that the implementation will be a breeze from a governance, management, and change point-of-view for the client. Sell your projects with the appropriate level of services in these areas. Recognize that you may need a full-time, on-site component of your team at the client for a large portion if not all of the project. And work with your senior management and sales professionals to help them understand that selling a project short in these areas will impact margins, project success, client satisfaction, and renewals.

Gary Schaumburg, Services Advantage

111 How to Control the Velocity of Payment

You never get a sale you don't ask for. In many cases, simply stating that 'our terms are payment in full or a percentage of total at time of agreement' will generate a check without further discussion. So either ask for payment in advance or provide an incentive for prompt payment. The benefit is fewer write-offs, significantly reduced time spent trying to get payment and greatly improved cash-flow.

I took this advice and applied it - we took the incentive route. I have found that when I ask, the client will pay up-front or purchase time before it is delivered and I rarely have disputes over the pre-paid work.

Alan Waitt, Director of services, Advanced Solutions International

112 Incentive Plans for a Product Sales Team

A friend of mine says that sales representatives are "coin operated". Tell them how they can earn more coins and they will do what you want them to do. He is a very wise man and so very right! I have found that the best way to get your services business off the ground is to handsomely reward the sales team through their compensation package in year one to sell services. At one company, I set up a program that paid the sales team 2X commission on any services sale. This clearly got their attention and helped to quickly change their behavior. Another technique that I have implemented in partnership

The best way to get your services business off the ground is to handsomely reward the sales team to sell service.

with the head of sales is to put a penalty clause in place in the sales representative's compensation package that automatically triggers 50% commission payout on the deal if they discount services at all. I believe that getting sales compensation right is the key to building and sustaining a successful services business inside of a product company. You have to partner closely with the head of sales to get the services business off the ground. Paying more in year one or in a year where you have new services to bring to market pays off handsomely in the long run by the increase in first year sales.

Valerie Osinski, Vice President Global Services, Kronos Inc.

113 How Do You Get Sales to Sell Services?

The greatest opportunity and the biggest challenge to getting your services business off the ground in a product company is to get your product sales team to understand and sell your services. Having built a services business at two SaaS companies, I have found that the best way to get your product sales team to understand and sell services is to package and price them as if they were a very discrete product offering. That means to put boundaries around the services and offer them in pre-established packages with a set price. It helps take the ambiguity out of it for the product sales team and they don't have to relearn how to sell or position. I have built packages to support our product for implementation, training, support services and analytic services. I have used a Silver, Gold, and Platinum naming convention. The services offered as well as the price tag for the packages goes up with each level. I have found this technique very successful and the sales team easily understands the offerings which makes them more likely to confidently position them with the customers.

Engage your product sales team by packaging your services.

Valerie Osinski, Vice President Global Services, Kronos Inc.

114 Negotiating Discounted Daily Rates

Most Software Sales folks or PS Engagement Managers will give away a discount on a PS day rate if pushed by the prospect and if it is within their discount authority.

Rule number 1 in negotiating is to always ask for something in return when you give something away. There is usually something you could ask for: hourly billing instead of daily billing, payment up-front, daily expense allowance instead of having to send actual receipts, cancellation fees. Make a list of what you want and give it to the guys on the front line along with the discount approval matrix.

Alistair Roe, VP, Services, EMEA, Mercury Interactive

115 Project Pricing

Clients want the most risk-free price proposal possible, where you assume the risk for slight changes in scope or project overruns. It's important to be creative, as you try to accommodate their wishes. Most people will listen to reason if appropriately presented.

A case in point involved a major east coast media ecommerce system. The client insisted on not-to-exceed pricing. They backed off to fixed price. We, however, were not satisfied with this approach because it left us too exposed to their failings or shortcomings. In the end we got them to agree to a fixed-price scoping and requirements phase, after which we used those requirements as the basis for a fixed-price development phase. Here, however, is where we got creative. Since they insisted on driving the testing phase of the project, we insisted that be time and materials. This turned out to be a prudent strategy, as they overran testing by 4 months. We had nearly a full team on-site during that period.

Avoid simply going with a simple and/or client-required pricing model.

An important caveat: This was a very friendly client with no shortage of trust and rapport on both sides. However, money and cost overruns can make strange bedfellows. When pressed by upper management, they tried to turn on us claiming that we really were not finished with the development phase when we said we were. They attacked that from multiple angles. We, however, kept a historical record of when modules were developed, and what changes were made after testing, in the source-code repository.

They tried to steamroll us but we prevailed in the end. We had $1.5 million at risk which we were able to recoup.

There were really two safeguards/tricks. One was tight language in the Statement of Work defining how end of development would be determined and signed-off. And, two, keeping historical records of everything we did.

And remember, when large revenue and expenses are at stake, even the best of customers can turn on you.

John Sullivan, Sr. Manager, SRA International

116 Bundles of Hours

We had a strategic goal to increase the total dollar value of each consulting deal sold as part of an initial implementation without pricing ourselves out of any deals. We hit upon the idea of offering "bundles of hours" that could be purchased by our clients before they had a specific project in mind – typically after the initial implementation. Of course, these bundles of hours were offered at preferential rates and had to be used within one year.

In the first deal where we presented this offering, the client requested estimates for future projects in years 2 and 3 of their relationship with us (year 1 being the initial implementation project which we had already scoped in detail). As the client was unsure of the exact scope of these potential future projects, we suggested they consider the bundles of hours approach. The client immediately latched on to this idea and agreed to contract for the largest bundle of hours for years 2 and 3 – adding over $200k to the deal that they were contracting for.

Build backlog by selling services hour bundles.

The same approach also worked well in contract renewal situations: again the client may not have a specific project in mind, but they know they are likely to do a number of projects with us. The beauty of this model is that they get budgetary approval for the expenditure in advance and then have a contracted bank of hours which they can draw upon as each project comes up. The benefits of this approach are that it:

- Avoids a lengthy contracting process for each small PS deal (reducing cost of sale);
- Reduces client objections to doing the project in the first place – after all, the dollars are already there and approved;
- Avoids the appearance that the client is being 'nickled and dimed' for smaller consulting services. We just draw against the bundle of hours they have already committed to, which is usually far less objectionable than having to get sign-off for more spending;
- Encourages the client to keep using professional services --- increasing total revenue and their "stickiness" to us as their vendor.

And what's more, the sales team likes the approach too. If they like it, it will start to get positioned and sold, which means less heavy lifting for the PS team!

Caroline Paxman, SVP Professional Services

117 Technique for Maintaining Billing Rates

Occasionally I find myself in the position of having provided an implementation proposal with the level of effort estimate (usually in terms of a range) and cost, but the overall number is more than what is needed to get the deal signed off. Since we often get follow-on work from our customers, I am extremely reluctant to discount rates since most likely I will have to live with that rate for that customer.

If there is no possibility of reducing the scope or getting the customer to take on additional responsibilities, one technique I have used is to include some non-billable time up-front and not charge for the time associated with an activity that would get me within the desired amount, for example: requirements analysis or a block of training.

> 🕮 **To maintain your bill rates, if all else fails, provide non-billable tasks to get the deal.**

While we still invoice the other activities at our standard rates, I highlight to the customer the effective rate he would be getting for this particular engagement. In this way, I am able to bill follow-on engagements at our standard rates.

Mark Janosy, VP Professional Services, Silvon Software

118 A Good Book to Read

Read Alan Weiss's book "how to maximize fees in professional service firms" for 57 tips and 52 pages of wisdom.

Alan Waitt, Director of Services, Advanced Solutions International

7. Services Delivery

This chapter covers topics such as resource management, code review, outsourcing, quality assurance, and support.

"I'm pleased to report that our project is ahead of schedule and under budget... not bad for the first hour!"

119 Keep Your Enemies Closer

We kicked off a major CRM project with a large Midwest retailer. At the first bump in the road, the client Project Director calls and complains to the Executive VP of Services (two levels above myself, a Director at the time). We pacified the situation and moved forward. I had previously established a 7:30 AM weekly Friday call with the client Project Director. During our next Friday call, I said the following, "David, in order to team effectively, I request that you allow me the opportunity to succeed before you make that call again." David hemmed and hawed and changed the subject.

David never called up the management chain again, and the project proved quite successful. We co-presented at the annual User Conference, and David and I actually developed a solid rapport. The retailer also signed up for additional services and provided references for our prospects.

Michael J. Lopez, Practice Director, SalesForce.com

120 Never Mess with a Production Instance

One of the basic rules I have with my team is that we never mess with a production instance of our customer's software! One of my consultants, despite several warnings, applied a patch into a production environment that corrupted several weeks of data. We had to pay the price dearly for this, but lesson learned and re-iterated is "Do not touch the customer's production instances"!

Arun Anur, Senior Practice Director, Oracle

121 It's Not Our Fault, But It is Our Problem

Preaching ownership and practicing ownership are two very different activities. Customers often preach ownership, but neglect to practice it. If your success measures are dependent on successfully implementing your software product to meet customer requirements, then issues created by the customer are your problem. Do not avoid them, just go ahead and own them. That is – document them, manage them to resolution, report on them and engage whoever you need to resolve them including (but not limited to) your boss, your boss' boss, your customer project manager's boss, the executive sponsor, your spouse, your dog and/or the mailman. You should do this as soon as you are aware there will be obstacles to resolution. Practice ownership and produce a win-win, successful implementation and a very happy customer.

Practice ownership and produce a win-win, successful implementation.

Debbie Stovall, VP, Professional Services, SumTotal Inc.

122 Look Beyond Implementation Services

I encourage you all to look beyond only offering the obvious implementation and training services as you evolve your services business. I have found in order to continue to grow our services revenue, I have had to develop strategic service offerings to add to the services portfolio. For example, we have a great opportunity as a SaaS provider to analyze our customer's data and come up with great business impact services that are geared toward solving an acute business pain for our customer. We have developed, as one example only, a strategic sourcing offering that allows us to have very strategic conversations with CXO level executives about how they are spending their sourcing dollars and how we can help them better target campaigns to attract candidates. These services are offered at a much higher price point than our implementation and training services because we are solving a very acute business pain. It takes our services out of being a "commodity" and up-levels them significantly. My main point here is to encourage you to look for opportunities to take your services to the next level whenever you can. When you do...it will pay off.

Valerie Osinski, Vice President Global Services, Kronos Inc.

123 Implications of Using the SaaS Model

In the old model, PS organization charters typically defined the responsibilities for promoting, selling, managing, and improving execution related to customer implementations. In the SaaS model, you may find yourself with responsibility for not just implementations, but also other customer-specific activities. The difference is far reaching, impacting your planning and resource management because most of these customer-specific activities will be non-billable.

In old model implementations, your customer-specific configurations, interfaces, loading, and most maintenance resided on the customer premises. After you completed your paid engagement, you'd transfer descriptions of the implementation to your Customer Support organization, but the physical solution itself became the customer's responsibility going forward. In the SaaS model, you may have many "customer-specific", implementation-related, configurations, data stores, and interfaces that reside within your company's environment forever more after your team is long done with the project. Who "owns" these? Is an upgrade to your interface infrastructure which includes customer-specific mappings an IT or a PS issue? If you're upgrading internally from one data schema to another who owns transfer of all customer data? Are these shared teams and shared responsibilities? Does IT Operations have responsibility for any customer-specific maintenance and/or changes?

In the SaaS model, you may find yourself with responsibility for not just implementations, but also other customer-specific activities.

The customer-specific tasks within a SaaS company can be monumental, especially if the company is going through frequent upgrades, acquisitions, or product introductions. It will serve you well to understand what your charter includes to be able to plan ahead. In your corporate plan, PS, Customer Support, IT, Operations, and Product organizations must work together to agree on who owns and supports customer-specific resource needs.

Gary Schaumburg, Services Advantage

124 Understand the Effect of Changes

Some years ago while implementing a new ERP system, the VP of engineering decided that he wanted to change the way the Bills of Material were put into the system. He had just been to a seminar where the experts said that the Bills should be shallow with deep routings. We tried to explain that this was not necessarily the best way to do this in a real implementation. He was adamant about this and proceeded with the change. Once the implementation was complete and the application had been running for a month we needed to make the first modification to the Bill of Material. Because of his change it was now realized that a change that required only one modification in the old way of recording the BOM would now take 30 changes under the new design. The result was that we had to go back and redo all of the Bills of Material, which delayed the complete sign-off of the project by an additional month.

📖 Understand the effect of changes before you make them.

Dan Catbagan, Sr. Enterprise Architect, Oracle Corp.

125 Hot Tips for Being Stuck in a Blizzard

I recently had the pleasure of being stuck in a blizzard in Denver which shut down the airport for 3 days. I managed to get home and documented the following tips if you should ever find yourself in a similar situation:

Always check the weather forecast when traveling during the winter. If there is a major storm coming, like say one of the biggest in 100 years, don't get on the plane. If the time frame is also around the holidays when flights are unusually full, totally blow it off.

📖 Escape from Denver: Tactics for avoiding trip delays during bad weather.

As soon as you think an airport is on the verge of being shut down, immediately buy Amtrak tickets for the next possible train out of town. This is the only sure fire way of transportation in inclement weather.

If traveling to a state where you are likely to have inclement weather, keep a list of limo services that cater to the business crowd. When things go bad, you don't want to compete for regular taxis.

At the first point you realize you may be trapped somewhere, immediately rent a 4 wheel drive if you can. This may come in handy down the road. If you are comfortable driving in the snow, you can usually "get out of Dodge" as soon as the plows have cleared the roads.

Do not stay out by the airport during a blizzard unless absolutely necessary. Staying downtown where food and other essential services are guaranteed is a better move.

If you happen to find a person who will drive you around and has a 4 wheel drive, tip very well so you get preference down the line. Chances are, you will need them again.

Make multiple, refundable reservations on flights so you have options once the airport opens. If you find there are no flights, try searching for first class tickets. You would be surprised how many more tickets magically appear.

Find out where other stranded people are going to drink and go there. The bonding that happens in stressful situations like this can actually be fun as everyone is having a shared experience.

If the main airport in town is closed, immediately check every other airport in the general area. The smaller ones may open sooner as they have less real estate to plow. Find out what airlines fly in and out of that airport and try to secure a flight anywhere at all.

If an airport opens up and there aren't lots of people there due to bad road conditions and lack of taxis and cars, go for it.

Don't listen to random, uninformed people; follow your gut.

I hope these tips help and get you home as soon as possible. Happy traveling.

Jason Rothbart, VP, Professional Services, newScale

126 Work Your Way Out of a Job

Jack Welch is famous for saying that successful employees should work themselves out of a job. This always struck me as a bit counterintuitive—making your job irrelevant seems more like a path towards unemployment than success. The truth is that rather than working yourself out of a job, you should take your current tasks and turn them into things that are easier to perform. In time, you will elevate yourself within the organization, as your insight and expertise will be better spent doing something else.

> **Rather than working yourself out of a job, you should take your current tasks and turn them into things that are easier to perform.**

This philosophy is very relevant in motivating and managing resources in a professional services organization. With the amount of concern focused on the offshoring of consulting jobs and increasing automation of services, this philosophy is particularly valuable today. I believe that the services world will flourish as the more mundane tasks are outsourced and services professionals move towards higher value and more interesting work. In any organization, the best way to motivate resources is to stress that the goal isn't to simply keep busy, but to figure out ways to make the business more efficient. This has the virtuous impact of helping people grow professionally and personally while also encouraging a culture where employees are mindful of costs. Pushing responsibility to the people closest to a business problem does wonders for an organization and does wonders for morale.

Morris Panner, CEO, OpenAir

127 High-Performing Project Teams

Impossible to imagine, but not everyone is cut out for managing projects. We made this observation several years ago when we started formalizing our project management process and began appointing individuals to manage projects who excelled at project management tasks. Prior to this change, we assigned the management of individual projects to just about anyone who had time in their schedule. You can imagine the range of results we experienced!

We saw an immediate positive effect when we changed to assigning projects to qualified project managers. Project schedules were better controlled. Communication within each project team improved. Clients were no longer left wondering about the status of their projects or making unrealistic assumptions. We also discovered that team performance improved as there was increased consistency in project team members from project to project.

Today, we have identified and implemented enduring cross-functional project teams. Each team is led by a highly skilled and fully qualified Team Leader, who manages all the projects and the schedules of his or her team members. Each team delivers a variety of projects, ranging in scope from small custom programming projects to complete turnkey ERP implementations. Team members generally work primarily on projects for their own team. This consistency has helped to build high-performing teams, as each member learns the strengths, weaknesses and roles of the other members.

We have identified and implemented enduring cross-functioned project teams.

Our team organization has been extended to the assignment of each client to a specific project team. As a result of this client assignment, the team members learn details about each client's business, which further improves the quality and efficiency of the services we deliver. The client assignment also helps with the sales process because we can involve the project team in the scoping and scheduling of proposed projects. Taking this concept one step further, some clients with sufficient volumes of work have requested dedicated project teams just for them. We have concluded that cross-functional teams are good for our business and provide a high-performing delivery team to the client.

Daniel Peyron, VP of Professional Services, Shaker Computer & Management Services, Inc.

128 A Key to Project Success

A key to project success is for the Customer to focus on his/her internal organization's readiness and communication while the consultant team focuses on project deliverables and the technology solution.

> A key to project success is for the Customer to focus on his/her internal organization's readiness and communication.

If I were to stack-rank the approximate 100 projects that I have been responsible for in over 10 years of service management by relative success from the customers' perspective they would line up for the most part in the order by which the customer focused on their own organization's readiness. The successes and failures I have seen due to organizational readiness have been remarkable.

One of the best examples of success is a vehicle manufacturer that wanted to build an on-line sales channel. By involving their dealers very early in the project they made them part of the project and owners in its success. The Project Team created an application process for the dealers to be accepted into the project. Dealers that were not a good fit were turned down. The remaining chosen dealers even paid for the project. During the rollout there was constant communication with the dealers about the progress of the project. Training was made available several times and a dynamic presentation was given at the dealer's national convention. The customer's internal project managers focused on this side of the project and did a wonderful job. They monitored the progress of the service team but let the consultants make the technology decisions. The project was a huge success and drove on-line business to their dealers.

In contrast, another customer of mine spent a lot of time and money on a very ambitious internal order forecasting system for several hundred store locations. The customer project team was so focused on the complexities of the technical architecture that they never really focused on user readiness. In the end, the system was delivered and met all requirements. However the stores did not receive adequate training to use the new system; the distribution centers did not have adequate integration to the system, and IT was not ready to support the system. The customer was forced, due to budget constraints, to release the consulting team with the message that once these pieces were in place the system would be switched on. It never was.

The lesson here, although not always entirely in your control, is to encourage your customer to focus on the internal communication and readiness necessary for a successful implementation. Give your customer confidence that your team with their supervision can deliver the technology and that his/her work of communication and involving the business users within their own company is the most valuable contribution they can make to the success of the project.

Eric Hansen, Engagement Manager, SalesForce.com

129 Project Reviews to Better Manage Resources and Demand

Why is it that every new project needed to start last week, with the best team you could possibly assign to it? It's like a broken record. On Monday you're told the project is on track to start in 30 days. On Tuesday, you need 5 people ready to go in 3 days. WHAT?! The life of a resource or delivery manager isn't easy. Everyone wants everything yesterday.

We were struggling with resource shortages in a hot employee market, and while working avenues to staff up to our proposed demand, we realized we had little control and oversight into the project pipeline. It wasn't clear who was deciding what projects were important and what the priority was. Or at least it wasn't well known how it was being done.

> 📖 We developed a project review process chaired by a project review committee.

We took this as a clue that we needed to get some order in the court. We developed a project review process chaired by a Project Review Committee (PRC). This committee was made up of a cross section of leaders from the organization who were empowered to make decisions. Further review was not necessary. The review process forced communication and synchronization within our organization and led to better planning. Rules for project reviews were created, and no out of band "approvals' were allowed. This was the key to the success. IT HAS TO BE ENFORCED!

We began to weigh the merits of each project based on information entered into a Project Review Template. This template was completed prior to the presentation by the project sponsor. We would determine if the timeline was flexible and make staffing recommendations based off the forecast. Once approved, a project sponsor no longer had to keep forcing the project to the front to be sure it got staffed. If it was approved, it was considered a priority for staffing.

Over time, the PRC became the defacto governing body within the company and became a highly adopted and respected process for project initiation, approval, and staff resourcing to a project. Without it, we'd all have walked the plank a long time ago.

The short message: Create a team of cross departmental leaders who review projects in order to allocate resources to the right projects. Respect the process and live by it. Don't go out of band. The right decision makers need to be there so decisions are final.

The result: Much higher visibility into our staffing issues and project pipeline. High adoption and higher project sponsor satisfaction. Less project/resource "churn."

Steven Giangregorio, Professional Services/Operations Executive

130 Avoid the Ivory Tower

When developing our methodology for service delivery for the first time, I embarked upon an organizational design by which we had 'back office' consultants led by a Director design and develop templates for service delivery. While this design seemed appropriate at first (don't burden the client-facing staff with administrative work), I soon learned about the flaws in my assumptions. Since the 'back office' team did not have the war-wounds of our field consultants, the recommendations and methodologies that they put forth were not embraced. Their credibility for providing tools to enhance productivity was suspect, regardless of the validity of their ideas. It was clear that this 'impedance mismatch' between those that do vs. those that design was insurmountable, so I distributed the methodology creation function out to our field consultants. They contributed to this effort between billable assignments and off-hours. The resultant work products were very well-embraced, and are not viewed as an 'Ivory Tower' professorial piece that is not based in real-world practical experience.

Bob Boehnlein, Executive Vice President, Global Services, Aprimo, Inc

131 Standardize on Reality

There is a lot of debate about whether organizations need a Project Management Office (PMO) or not. Is it an unnecessary overhead expense? Is it a strategic advantage in the marketplace? The answer to these questions is always company specific. Our organization, a PS department inside a software product company, decided standardization of project delivery was required to maintain consistency and project margin expectations. With the USA being such a large territory, how best to launch a standard platform was the base challenge. The organization had established project managers and ongoing projects so introducing a brand new way of doing things was not a cost-effective option.

> **Our organization decided standardization of project delivery was required to maintain consistency and project margin expectations.**

The answer – get contributions from everyone and those become the base owned by the users. A scrub of duplicate document types and reviews by management narrowed the selection to the standard set for deployment. A quick formatting fix and we had a base of process and templates ready in a short period. Yes, it all sounded great until we ran into the biggest lesson learned possible: A Project Management Office is only as powerful as the management supporting it and the use of its standardized assets by the organization. Adoption is something that doesn't happen overnight and needs constant oversight to ensure it is happening. Who doesn't take a shortcut now and then by recopying old documents from their hard drive instead of pulling the new templates from a company website? How do you break old habits? No matter how much reality you try to insert into standards, you are always making someone change and that's what you must realize. Get commitment for project oversight from key resources and management support that standards are important and necessary to benefit the overall productivity of the organization. The project reviews put in place help emphasize the use of templates and continue to reinforce the adoption rate to this day. Reality is always more challenging than the theory behind it – recognize this early and incorporate reality into your standardizations.

Jodi Cicci, Global Project Management Director, Software AG

132 Managing Remotely within Professional Services

I have spent the last 6 years being a remote manager (as in located on the opposite coast from our headquarters office) of a remote team (as in managing consultants based all over the East coast) with remote peers (as in also not based at Corporate).

So, how does one manage such remoteness without becoming aloof?

In its best form, being remote creates a sense of independence (akin to managing your own business) with a side benefit of being removed from the daily gossip mill of the corporate office. But at the opposite end, that same distance can create a world of isolation, lack of awareness of important decisions, and the need to put extra effort into building and sustaining relationships with your co-workers.

> 🕮 **When you are remote, make an extra effort to stay connected.**

Here are some actions to consider:

It is a good practice for PS Management to send out bi-weekly updates on the latest company initiatives, decisions, changes, etc., to all consultants.

Hold regular team meetings, where the information flow is bi-directional.

Do not assume that people have access to information – it's better to provide extra information, than to omit it.

The administrative challenges for on-the-road consultants are far greater than for employees at corporate. The processes defined for managing administrative matters must be reviewed and adjusted to bring effectiveness to the remote team.

Set up internal projects to allow "cross-pollination" across groups, and allow consultants to reach across organizational boundaries. This creates an expanded support group, and a greater sense of belonging to the company at large.

Carve out time for developing and maintaining Knowledge Management systems, and building the importance of these systems into consultants' performance plans.

Catch up with your consultants, talk about the project at hand, outlook for future projects and find out what's going on with the consultant in general.

Make an extra effort to be in touch with co-workers, subordinates and superiors, even if you do not need something from them at this moment.

Communicate up and down that you rely on information flow from your own superiors and co-workers.

Establish relationships with people across the organization, so that you have more of a view of what is happening outside your individual small world.

And last, but not least, make sure to organize team events (regional holiday dinners, etc.) that include remote employees. And if your company cannot afford such regional events, then let all your remote employees know that they are invited, in spirit, to the corporate gatherings. Avoiding the social aspects of "I wasn't invited to dinner" can go a long way.

Olga Brown, former Actuate Regional Professional Services Manager

133 Using New Terminology to Facilitate Change

While customers always have the best intentions of making the changes required with their new system, it's often difficult to get them to do so. One way to move the process along is to change the business terminology, using words and phrases more inline with the strategic objectives of the new solution. This helps get the customer out of their old mindset, and ease the change process.

A few years back, we used such an approach to help facilitate significant change at a large mortgage bank. The bank had a very risk-centric approach to their partners and customers, which was reflected in their customer-facing systems. We were tasked with implementing a new system justified by a customer-focused, sales-driven business case. To help drive the necessary changes, we started using new and different terminology. We started to refer to "brokers" as "customers" or "partners". Instead of talking about "loans", we talked about "deals". We started using terms like "win the business" when talking about the bank's interactions with their customers. Eventually we helped the customer to stop thinking about each transaction as a risk-laden event, but as an opportunity to sell, to satisfy a customer and to grow their business.

This transformation was exemplified in the solution we delivered. It made doing business with our customer easier and more efficient, driving a solid increase in sales and customer satisfaction. And along the way, we received a great degree of buy-in from those on the customer side responsible for implementing the change.

Dan Martino, Practice Director, MortgageHub Advisory Services

134 How to Get Customers to Pay for Project Management

Anyone who has been working in the Professional Services business for any length of time knows that the key to a successful services engagement is a good Project Manager. However, it is usually the first thing a client will complain about having to pay for and conversely the first thing that a client will blame for a project's failure.

To address this issue we have moved towards fixed price SOWs that include a description of project management services along with all other deliverables for a bottom line price and estimated hours. But not all clients are willing to go with fixed-price contracts. Some customers prefer time-and-material contracts. What do you do in that case? We do the same thing for our hourly SOWs as we did for fixed price. We provide a bottom line price and estimated hours.

Some customers may ask for specifics but our experience is that most do not. For those who do, we discuss the value of Project Management and verbally communicate estimated hours. By bundling all deliverables and providing a bottom-line price, focus is placed on their budget and not on any specific line item.

Peter J. Sa, Vice President, Professional Services,
Lakeview Technologies

8. Offshoring

This chapter covers topics such as the challenges of managing offshore teams, retention and motivation of offshore teams, how and when to leverage offshore resources, and offshore models.

"Please continue to hold. All of our representatives are currently busy luring jobs away from your country."

135 Communication Between Onshore and Offshore Teams

One of the most important factors in making an offshore strategy work for PS projects is good communication. Regular interaction and the right level of communication between team leads on both sides is a key ingredient in making projects with offshore resources successful. There are several communication models to choose from, and the choice depends on multiple factors. The factors include project duration, team size, onshore/offshore resource split, level of detail and documentation, extent of requirement changes during the construction phase of the project and the level of participation from the onshore team leads to work with offshore team leads, etc.

One of the models we are implementing, which shows promise, is the use of liaison engineers in the US office. This model solves the problem of requiring every key member of the project team to sacrifice his/her personal life and be on-line and/or on-call with offshore counterparts at odd hours. This is especially challenging on PS projects where the expectation is for the key members to work with offshore teams outside local business hours and work with customers and the onshore team members during regular business hours. The approach mitigates the risk of offshore projects being successful based on personal sacrifice made by key project team leads and their families!

> **One model which seems to show positive signs is the use of liaison engineers.**

In a couple of cases, we have selected senior members of the offshore team to play the role of liaison engineer. These engineers, now based in our West coast office, act as glue on the projects between the US-based teams and the India-based teams. Because the engineers were previously part of the offshore team this approach ensures good bonding with the offshore team members. Being in the corporate head office fosters closer relationships with onshore team members.

During the construction phase, the liaison engineer gets clarification of requirements, explanations of bugs and conveys changes in priories to offshore teams, etc. With this model, we are aiming to make one of the key promises of the offshoring model come true for our customers – efficient around-the-clock global software delivery!

Dilip Shah, VP, Professional Services Engineering, Dorado Corp.

136 Offshore Staff Retention: Invest in the Individuals

Like most companies with an offshore facility in India, staff turnover was an ongoing problem. Attrition rates of 15% per annum and higher were common. The attrition was killing us. On one of my visits to this office, we did some soul-searching with our local managers. We came up with a powerful strategy for managing our offshore resources.

One common pool: we had three distinct technical groups and managed them independently as silos. We changed to a 'single pool' concept, treating the entire center as a single pool of resources. We now have product developers performing short-term stints in services (6 months or less) and traveling overseas to those assignments. Services staff members are available for product development projects. Result: improved career growth options and varied work assignments.

Hire in batches: we're hiring batches of resources, 6 or more individuals at a time. The batch receives common training, and the individuals are then chosen for the best-fit assignments. This is the practice of the larger companies, and it works just as well for smaller companies. It adds to the variability of the career path and creates a sense of camaraderie.

> **We did some soul-searching with our local managers and came up with a powerful strategy for managing our offshore resources.**

Scheduled rotations: we're rotating new hires through head-office within their first year of employment. Rotations run from a few weeks to 3 months, depending on their visa status. The rotations are planned on a 12-month rolling schedule. This creates a sense of anticipation and a greater desire to ramp-up in time for meeting the HQ counterparts.

Long-term relocation: The opportunity to relocate with their families is a tangible bonus for our offshore staff. And this bonus differentiates us from many of the neighboring tech companies, leading to greater loyalty and easier recruiting efforts. There are costs involved for us, but this is worth the investment

Work Culture: interestingly, we found that our unstructured work environment is a significant asset. It seems that other companies are highly structured, with 8-to-6 mentalities. On my last visit, we heard of companies that turn off the power at 6pm, and that charge the employee for personal phone calls. I'll confess --- I have no idea when my team comes into the office or how many personal calls they make. But I do know they turn around their assignments quickly.

Overall, our offshore facility has been a significant asset, one that I promote in our sales cycle. Thinking of these resources as a close part of our team and not as remote resources makes all the difference.

Joe Longo, VP Professional Services, MetricStream

137 Offshore Retention and Motivation

Retention and motivation of an offshore team are some of the major challenges companies face when they utilize an offshore strategy. In India the current hiring environment is very competitive and is similar to the Silicon Valley hiring boom of the 90s.

We have been using an offshore strategy for professional services and product development for 4 years. Approximately half of our Professional Services organization is in India. To minimize attrition and maximize motivation of our offshore team we:

Provide opportunities for team members to travel to the U.S. either for long-term (1 year) or short-term (90 days) visits depending on their purpose and what the resource is willing and able to do. For some, an engagement at the customer's site is attractive. Any visit to the

U.S. should include time at the company offices. This provides a great opportunity for the person to build rapport with US team members. If it is only a short visit, we typically schedule the visit during a project phase where interaction with the US team can be most beneficial and productive. We have found the design phase is a good time to bring team members over. It gives them the opportunity to be very involved in the design process and obtain project information that will help the team in India once they return and the project has moved into the implementation phase.

For resources interested only in a short-term visit, we set up a rotational plan where we bring over a few members at a time throughout the year. Resources interested in a long-term visit may also be interested in obtaining a Visa and living in the US for a more extended period. This can be an excellent opportunity to bring good talent into the company.

Retention and motivation of an offshore team is a major challenge.

US team member visits to India are also important for team building.

Provide a career path for team members. Provide opportunities that enable team members to grow their skills and advance their careers. For example, if they are initially involved only in implementation, assign them to a task that enables them to improve their design skills.

Recognize and reward the work of individuals and the team. There are a variety of ways you can do this, including financial rewards such as bonuses, stock options, or paid time off. We also include team tenure as one of the factors in our compensation plan to encourage team retention.

If the team has worked hours beyond the normal overtime expected, give them some time off. If you finish a major project and plan on taking the US project team out for lunch be sure you do something similar for the offshore team. If you have company t-shirts, be sure to send one to each member of the offshore team.

Most offshore vendors have their own programs for recognizing their employees. Be sure you are aware of these and provide input on key members of your team. Periodically let your team's manager know who is doing a good job.

Promote your company to the team. Make sure the team is aware of all the great things your company is doing, how your business is growing, and why the company is going places. Individuals want to be working for a growing, successful US company. Remember, if you are a small company you are competing for resources with much larger US companies who often provide better benefits.

Tanya Johnson, SVP, Engineering and Support, Avolent

138 Offshore Models

I have used two different models, "white box" and "black box", when working with an offshore partner. Both have been successful. The "white box" model provides more flexibility and control of offshore operations and deliverables than the "black box" model. It also requires a greater investment of time and involvement from members of your team. I have summarized the two models as follows:

"White Box" Model –The US team interacts directly with offshore team members. The project manager and technical lead assign and manage the tasks the offshore team works on. Weekly status meetings are held with both the US and offshore teams to review progress of the assigned tasks, make changes in assignments, and communicate other project information. Meetings with individuals on the team are held when needed. In addition to meetings, email and Instant Messenger are used to communicate with team members daily. There is also an offshore program manager who deals with the day-to-day operation of the offshore team including HR issues, equipment needs, and screening of potential new hires. The US team interviews and gives final approval of all candidates who are hired.

The offshore team is treated like an extension of the US team. It is held to the same standards and goals as the US team and follows the processes and methodology of the US team. They also utilize the same tools (e.g., bug tracking system). Since your team is interacting directly with offshore team members on a daily basis and can assess their skills, you can create well-balanced engagement teams made of both US and offshore individuals.

"Black Box" Model - In this model all communication and interaction with offshore team members is done through the offshore program manager. The program manager can be located in the US or offshore. The vendor program manager makes all hiring and management decisions. They provide direction to the offshore team, assign tasks to resources, and manage delivery. The team utilizes the systems and methodology of the vendor. You have no visibility into the day-to-day operations of the team and no interaction with the offshore team other than through the program manager.

Although I prefer the "white box" model because it provides more flexibility and control, I have been successful with both models.

Tanya Johnson, SVP, Engineering and Support, Avolent

139 Going Offshore

Investors in enterprise software product companies today almost always require a business model that leverages the cost effectiveness of offshore resources in countries like India and China. However, these companies need to be careful in how and when they leverage offshore resources for their nascent Professional Services organizations. Implementing projects with an immature product, while the implementation methodology is not repeatable, can be a recipe for failure.

Choosing the right time to go offshore is key to the deployment of offshore PS resources.

In the early stages of a company, the product is raw and usually requires significant product engineering in order to deliver a solution that meets the needs of the early adopters of the product. Each Professional Services engagement tends to be unique. Pioneering customers of the solution are often unclear of their requirements. They formulate their requirements as they build clarity around how the product will help their business objectives and as they start appreciating the changes that the solution will impose on their business operations. In this circumstance, it is critical to have a sharp business analyst, technical architect and project manager, who are typically the same person in Professional Services organizations of early stage companies, work on-site with the customer. This individual needs to stay close to the customer throughout the entire project and hence, for a US customer, cannot be offshore during any part of the project. Most companies realize this but attempt to minimize implementation costs by leveraging an offshore technical implementation team. The outcome is often an implementation that is poor in quality, late in delivery and non-conforming to the intended requirements of the customer. This is never a good outcome but especially distressing when a company is trying to win its first few referenceable customers.

The challenges encountered are attributable to:

Early implementations tend to be highly iterative. They require a team that is agile and can make swift course corrections as customer requirements crystallize. An offshore model makes this difficult.

Since the product functionality in early stage companies evolves rapidly and often specifically to meet the requirements of the customer, the implementation team has to work very closely with the product engineers to learn the product, to ingest the new functionality being developed and to collaborate to properly design the final solution as well as to diagnose and debug product issues that emerge. While many early stage companies do have engineering presence offshore, they often opt to put only the QA staff and developers of non-critical product functions offshore. Not being co-located with the core product development team undermines the efficacy of the offshore implementation team.

Hence nascent software companies should consider leveraging offshore resources for their Professional Services organizations after their product has stabilized to the point that it is not being customized for implementations and after the implementation process has become repeatable and well documented.

Arvind Singhal, VP, Worldwide Technical Support, Interwoven Inc.

140 Challenges in Offshore Implementation

Over the years, all of us have heard customers, consultants and vendors complain about the "problems" with the offshore model (although they like the cost arbitrage). This tip is not meant as a discussion of the challenges of the offshore model. However, I would like to highlight one area that most folks in the US and Europe tend to neglect.

In the traditional software implementation model, design specifications (functional and technical) are written by solution architects and are given to the application development programmers. With an onshore development model, during the "construction/coding" phase, if the programmer/developer has questions on the design, the architect was readily available for clarification and discussion. If the architect has questions, he/she would check with the client. This worked with good precision since everyone was co-located.

However, with the onset of the "offshore development" team, the work is now separated into the solution design work that happens onshore and the development work that happens offshore. In the new model, the solution architect sends the design specs to the offshore team for development. This is compounded by time zone differences, geographical separation, language and cultural differences. In this model, if programmers have questions, they cannot easily and readily go back for clarification to the Solution Architects.

To address the realities of offshore development, the level of detail (documentation) in the offshore model needs to be at a much more granular and detailed level than the onshore model. While this sounds logical, this is not the case with many companies. Companies who have mastered the offshore model with rigorous standards like CMMI, and Six Sigma understand this challenge.

The bottom line is to pay a lot of attention to the level of detail in all communication to and from the offshore center and the onshore team. Doing this will reduce downtime, increase throughput, increase team morale, and at the end of the day, enable the team to hit its project targets.

Sunny Kumar

141 Managing an Offshore Development Center

The perennial professional services question is "how do I raise my delivery margins, meet variable customer demands, keep bench time to a minimum and ensure high quality project delivery?" We're all faced with these questions every day. I have addressed these questions, at least in part, through utilization of an offshore development organization as a part of my delivery team. I have deployed this offshore model in two distinct versions, each with its own benefits and pitfalls.

So what are the two basic models? The two basic approaches are: 1. build a direct team of employees that you manage directly and 2. outsource the team to an in-country vendor (with an additional variation of managing the project team directly or outsourcing the project and management to the outsource vendor). Both models can work well in the correct environment. I won't get into the advantages and pitfalls here, but focus instead on the basic requirements that are necessary in either model to manage effectively.

The number one success factor for managing an offshore development process is a formal communication plan.

The number one success factor for managing an offshore development process is a formal communication plan. Managing project development/delivery to customer specifications on-site can be a challenge but add into that mix multiple development locations away from the customer, in different time zones and with some measure of cultural difference and the results can be disastrous without a pre-defined communication process. Here's an outline of required elements (not all inclusive and can vary based on the maturity of the team, the on-site project manager, project complexity, etc.):

1. On-site project manager/consultant that works with the customer to clearly define the functional requirements of the solution. This functional specification must be "signed off" as accurate by the customer and establishes the initial scope of the development effort.

2. Transmittal of the functional specifications to the development team key contact/architect to define the technical specifications (I have also seen this step done on-site by a technical architect, but often co-location with the developers makes this process run more smoothly).
3. Detailed technical specifications are then defined, taking into account the offshore resources, their maturity, experience and technical skills as well as the end solution required.
4. The technical specifications are then returned to the on-site manager/consultant for customer review and sign-off. This should include agreement on the development timeline as well.
5. Establish a regular schedule of code/solution reviews with the on-site manager/consultant and the customer. These can be set as frequently as the development cycle permits but must happen regularly during the development process (NOT JUST PRIOR TO FINAL DELIVERY!).
6. Upon final code/project review and delivery there should be some form of formal acceptance testing by the customer, with support from the offshore developers. This should generate acceptance of the project, once any required bug fixes are implemented.

There are a few other tools that can make the offshore process more effective. These tools include a common change management tool and a common development process/methodology (check-in, check-out, peer review, test plans, etc.). It is also quite useful to have a common content management solution to manage project documents, specifications, etc. Project documents should all adhere to common standards with standard templates for all documents.

Strong project management is required on both ends of the process to ensure effective and timely project delivery and customer expectations management. This includes agreement and management to a single project schedule.

These are only a few of the factors to consider, but can form the basis of a very effective addition to your project teams.

Michael Fauscette, VP, Software Applications Research, IDC

142 Offshore Outsourcing – Understanding the Challenges

Prompted by the huge media exposure and the promise of lower cost and other benefits, a large number of companies have embarked on offshoring. Many are experiencing significant challenges. Better than 50% of offshoring initiatives fail to meet original expectations.

📖 It's important to understand the major challenges of offshoring.

However, companies can and many do realize significant benefits through offshoring. Planning, executing and continued oversight of an offshore strategy requires a lot of hard work, long-term orientation and management competence, bandwidth and commitment.

To begin with you need to understand the major challenges of offshoring. I have broken them down into two categories – Internal and External.

Internal Challenges

Unrealistic expectations - Often companies overestimate savings and underestimate the effort and cost of establishing and managing the relationship. You need to invest the time up-front to gain a realistic understanding of both; once done, it is important to communicate to all stakeholders.

Improper project selection - You need to clearly define project selection criteria; in particular whether you plan to offshore projects that require direct customer interaction by the offshore team.

Governance - How do you plan to organize the offshoring function? In addition to technical management, how do you manage the business and relationship issues? How do you plan to measure if the effort is successful?

Processes - Recognize that vendor processes for development and integration may be different than yours; reconcile differences and establish a mechanism that is acceptable to both parties. The other major element is establishing processes for visibility and control.

External Challenges

Staffing and retention - Competition for the right skills in countries like India is very high; you need to determine whether the vendor has and can offer you the staff with the right level of experience. Once you establish a team, you need to proactively manage staff retention.

Time zone differences - Your staff in the US will need to get used to staying up late and/or coming in early for teleconferences with the offshore team.

Country and vendor infrastructure - Both can be issues; you need to determine if your project needs special tools and/or other infrastructure.

Security - Major offshore vendors have established good business practices, but if you are dealing with a small vendor you need to make sure that you are not risking your Intellectual Property.

Vendor stability - Thorough due diligence of vendor stability should be part of the vendor selection process.

Cultural differences - This is a significant issue; training programs to help you understand how culture affects communications and your projects are available.

Geo-political concerns - This should be taken into account during vendor selection. Once a relationship with a vendor is established, it is hard to change.

Distance to vendors - India, the most popular destination being 10,000 miles away means it takes an entire day to reach your vendor. Travel to the vendor at regular intervals will be part of managing offshoring.

What does this mean and what can you do?

For competitive reasons, every company must determine if offshoring makes sense. If the decision is to go forward with offshoring, you need to recognize that it takes a lot of work. Understanding challenges is the first step. Management is key to success in offshoring. To ensure success, you should get a deeper understanding of offshoring best practices.

M. M. Sathyanarayan, President, Global Development Consulting, Inc.

143 Look Past Cost When Outsourcing

Many senior executives don't look past 'cost' and 'reputation' when considering an outsourcing alternative. I helped keep one company out of the ditch when they went offshore for Help Desk Services.

Before they settled on the lowest "cost" provider, I advised them to:

> 🕮 **You need to look beyond "cost" and reputation.**

Conduct a detailed Customer Satisfaction survey with both the key executives of the user group as well as a solid sample of the users.

They ended up performing a survey on a scale of 1 to 10 which ranked:

Time to take a call (service metric) – average and during month and quarter end closing cycles.

Time cycle to take the call, through first follow-up in which the Customer was given a status and expected 'fix/solve' date. (Time metric)

Time lapse between forecast fix date and actual release to Customer date. (Time metric)

Quality of Service representative taking the trouble ticket call. (Quality metric)

Did they dig for the facts and symptoms? Did they ask "what constituted success" for the fix? Did they commit to a status update? Did they meet their commitments for follow up? Did they experience any difficulty in understanding their service representative?

How quickly did they reproduce the issue (Time and Quality of Test Environment)

The framework for contract negotiations became:

Defined the existing Service Level Agreement between users and support/developers to define 'Business Down' criteria all the way to 'Nice to Have when you have time', as well as targets for resolution for each category. Gained a better understanding of current resolution times.

Quantified true cost of existing Service components:

Help Desk personnel, training requirements for new staff, existing cost for hardware and software to reproduce issues

Defined Customer Satisfaction metrics to maintain at least current satisfaction levels

Determined Time for Sustaining Engineering to forecast fix, forecast test and forecast release of patch

It was only then that both the outsourcer and the Customer were able to have a meaningful dialogue about expectations, costs, quality of service going forward and benchmarks for bonus and penalties for contract severance.

Bill Marshall, Owner, Marshall Management Consulting

9. Cross-Functional Alignment

This chapter covers topics such as alignment with sales, sharing resources across lines of business, understanding and reducing partner conflict, making customer support a strategic partner, and building strategic relationships.

"I want everyone at the meeting to dress up like Lego blocks. Then we can see exactly how each team member interlocks with the other team members in the project."

144 Good Reasons to Befriend Customer Support

Your friends in the customer support organization can be a strategic partner of your services team. They typically cover all of the same product skills as your team, have close ties to R&D, understand customer issues, have a good product training infrastructure established and are a primary custodian of the product knowledge base. You can find great synergies in the areas just listed and should look for opportunities to share these processes and infrastructure to make both teams more productive and effective. Customer Support can be an effective feeder organization to services. It is a great place for new hires to learn your products, customers and organization without the pressures of being in front of a customer and without eating into your margin. Customer support can also be a great way to give your road warriors a break; they can work in support when they need to spend some time at home.

> 📖 **Customer support can be an effective feeder organization to services.**

Mark Rask, Services Director, Lawson Software

145 Alignment with Sales

Alignment with sales at all levels is critical! As a leader your second most important step to success is to align your goals with the sales leadership. Once your goals are in alignment, the next step is to ensure the compensation plan rewards the sales reps to sell the services you can deliver. Treat your sales reps as if they are your most important customers! They won't always be right, but they will always be your path to setting the stage for a successful services engagement with your external customer. Spend time directly with the sales reps to ensure you understand the world from their eyes. Their perspective is invaluable in getting underneath the marketing and hype and seeing what you really need to tweak in your approach to drive higher product and services sales. Once the sales reps see you investing in them they will work harder with you and your team and you will have more fun.

Beth Martinko, VP Services, Wavelight

146 The Sales Rep Said What?

One of the most frustrating things in an implementation is to realize that the client's expectations are not in line with the capabilities of the product. This is often attributed to an overly aggressive sales team that seemingly "over promised", leaving the PS team feeling they are in the position of having to "under deliver".

Unfortunately, many services personnel will throw the sales team "under the bus" at this point and reset the client's expectations unilaterally. While likely effective in the short term (and may even increase the bond between the services team and the client), this is likely a pyrrhic victory. The client may start to lose respect for the solution/company as a whole and subsequent issues may be that much harder to resolve.

📖 **Actively work with the sales team to understand how the client's expectations were set.**

I have found the best approach (from having been on both sides of this fence) is to actively work with the sales team to understand how the client's expectations were set and then work with the sales team and the client to find an appropriate solution.

Often, this interaction will show that the sales team didn't over promise, they were simply told different requirements, or perhaps they have a different solution to the problem. Even if the sales team was a bit too optimistic, it is often best to resolve these issues from a company point of view (PS and Sales) rather than having PS try to do it alone.

Overall, the most important thing a services professional can do in situations like this is to remember the sales cycle never ends, it only evolves to the implementation phase and customer satisfaction is paramount.

Dale McConnell

147 Working with Fast-Paced Sales Groups

Our business was expanding rapidly in Europe, and managing customer expectations regarding engagement kickoffs and schedules was a challenge, to put it mildly. The principle problem was internal coordination between Sales and Services. Sales were off to the races and were not in sync with PS with respect to timing, schedules, and rollout expectations. Add in multiple languages, time zone issues with HQ located on the West Coast, and severe staffing constraints and we had a real problem. Sounds straightforward enough, but it proved to be challenging to re-set internally. Here are some things that helped address the "customer gaps" that were getting wider every day:

Sales PS Presentation - PS developed a detailed PowerPoint presentation that ALL Sales and Systems Engineer's used in the sales process. This presentation focused on proven basic product functionality with VERY limited customizations.

> 🕮 **If you manage the customer expectation process properly up-front, everything else will line up.**

In fact, we explicitly highlighted those customizations that should be considered in the presentation in an effort to guide, not limit PS work. We did this not to reduce the billable hours but rather to put a mechanism in place where we could:

Ramp the resources to support the growing backlog and

Get our sales force aligned with a more simplistic approach to get clients running sooner.

Assigned PS Project Manager - PS assigned a technical Project Manager to start work within 30 days of contract signing. This, while it wasn't 100% ideal for customers, proved to be a practical solution to:

- Set in motion the need to assemble a team from both sides - client and our company.
- Helped accelerate contract details.
- Drove consistency in managing expectations.

If you manage the expectation process properly with your customers up-front (especially in international venues) everything else lines up. Profits, resource management, generating real value for the client and most of all peace of mind for those of us balancing all of the above.

Jeff Jarvis, CEO, Agentek, Inc.

148 Working with Sales

How many times have you been confronted with a "must do" deal at the end of the quarter where the Professional Services team has not had the opportunity to fully understand the customer's requirements or special contract terms? With constant pressure to "make" the quarter, I've been forced to agree to deals where we lacked sufficient knowledge of the specifications and the customer's expectations.

One of the worst examples of an end of the quarter "shotgun" deal was with a very large, new customer. At the last minute a large systems integrator had to back out of the deal because the client was also their accounting client. We were faced with losing the deal or accepting blindly the proposal created by the systems integrator. We worked diligently through the contract terms with both legal departments and were able to change the SIs fixed-price bid into fixed price for only the initiation phase. The initiation phase was defined to include a detailed estimate for the development phase.

> **With 20/20 hindsight we should have insisted on a time-and-materials initiation phase.**

Although we lacked sufficient knowledge of the project and had not been involved in creating the SI's proposal, the client and the deal were critical enough to accept the risk of jumping into an unknown project with a tremendous amount of technical risk.

The initiation phase timeline, resources and budget took four times more effort than we had proposed. We lost a great deal of money with the potential to lose much more if we continued as the prime contractor. We were able to convince the client to substitute a large SI to program manage the next phase of the project.

With 20/20 hindsight we should have insisted on a time-and-materials initiation phase. The only way to effectively manage the client's insatiable appetite for scope expansion was through the pocketbook. We also should have insisted on a fully committed, knowledgeable and dedicated client project team with clear "ownership" for the project – this is extremely difficult to do in large complex organizations. We managed to overcome the client team deficiencies through constant communication, executive sponsorship and detailed project documentation. But the single most important "lesson learned" was to work closely with the sales team to define the requirements rather than being forced to blindly accept them after the fact.

Anonymous

149 SaaS - Internal Coordination is Key

The role of Professional Services organizations in Software-as-a-Service (SaaS) companies is similar on the surface to that within what I'll refer to as the "old" style, license model, on customer premises world. Many implementation responsibilities will look the same. But the most important differences have to do with the fact that aspects of the business which were "external" to the software company in the old model (single instance, one-off, on customer premises, affecting only one customer) become "internal" in the SaaS model (shared code base, shared infrastructure, affecting all customers at once, highly interdependent processes and policies). With this internalization comes a greater need for coordination, communication, and "getting it right the first time", across all company departments.

> **Make sure your company is comfortable with inter-group debate and decision making.**

The implications of this software world turned "outside in" are numerous and often subtle, but if you go down the path of trying to operate not only your PS group, but your Sales, Pre-Sales, Operations, Customer Support, and Product Development groups in any way like in the old model, you are bound to create irreversible problems. This has led to creation of a "customer operations" type role within many SaaS companies, with responsibility for managing coordinated execution.

Challenges tend to be fairly consistent across emerging SaaS companies. If you work for a more mature SaaS player, you've probably experienced these and solved them as a matter of survival already. But if you're running PS for one of the many SaaS startups being funded, my advice is to think carefully about how these might apply to your company and solution.

So, Tip #1 is: internal coordination is key. Make sure your company is comfortable with inter-group debate and decision making. Engage your senior management to foster an environment of straight talk and constructive conflict. Ensure there is an established way to create, modify, codify, or at least informally agree to the interdepartmental processes and policies that you'll need to put in place to be successful.

Gary Schaumburg, Services Advantage

150 Project Governance

A successful project governance structure requires representation from not only the customer's IT organization, but also from the business owners. It's unfortunate, but all too often we see projects funded, owned by, and managed solely by IT. Without proper oversight by the business, the likely outcome is a system that meets the requirements set forth by the IT organization, however, fails to deliver business value and a return on investment. While IT has only the best intentions, they often lack the intimate, detailed knowledge of the underlying business processes. Usability suffers and often the business process being automated becomes more convoluted and time-consuming than that of the original. This is particularly true in call center environments, where every second of call time counts.

A successful project-governance structure requires representation from not only the customer's IT organization, but also from the business owners.

To combat this, it is critically important to demand both IT and expert business user involvement from the outset of functional requirements definition all the way through system and performance testing. In packaged systems implementations, it is also critical to work closely with business users to maximize the use of native functionality and ensure that the requirements are not permitted to grow out of control with over-configuration.

How do you balance judicious configuration/custom development? The answer is an empowered and active steering committee with an agreed to mission, vision, and charter. The steering committee must have representation by all stakeholders -- IT, business, and systems integrators to be effective arbiters of difficult decisions that must be made on scope, configuration, budget considerations and project schedule.

There are myriad variables that can affect a business system implementation, but with the proper governance structure, you can help to control those variables and increase the probability of success.

Jim Siegel, VP, CRM Consulting Delivery, SAP America, Inc.

151 Sales and Services – Aligning for Success

The pressure is on technology companies to deliver ever-growing revenues, margins and market share, while simultaneously increasing operational efficiency and "doing more with less". As Professional Services leaders within our organizations, the inevitable questions must be answered: How do we build confidence and consensus with our counterparts in the sales organization? How do we insure we are involved in the sales cycle to position our offerings? How do we align for success?

Here are 3 fundamental strategies I've used to become a starter on my sales team:

Communicate – By nature, sales people are slightly paranoid, extremely possessive and generally risk averse. Regardless of the personality or approach, when a deal is in play they are interested in only one thing: how do I remove any barriers between me and a signed contract? When a sales person views Professional Services as a barrier you can be assured that you won't be invited to the dance.

By communicating the value proposition of your organization, through successes at other customer engagements and involvement with similar solutions, your stock will rise and your dance card will fill up quickly. Confidence starts with a single success.

Participate - When you are invited to the dance, be a leader. To arrive at the desired result you must be a driver in the process. This means more than periodic involvement or providing collateral for a meeting. Be present and proactive at every step in the process. By taking your share of ownership and accountability in the sales cycle, you are helping share the risk and reward. The sales team will love you for it.

How do we insure we are involved in the sales cycle to position our offerings? How do we align for success?

Differentiate - Now that you're a critical member of the sales team, it's time to shine. Remember that your organization has experience and knowledge that no other competitor has. Whether it is product or space specific, complex solution delivery, large project scope or creative delivery arrangements, there is ALWAYS a differentiator that separates you from the competition. When working to craft the delivery strategy, think outside of the box, even if it means branching into unfamiliar and uncomfortable territory. Providing the sales team and the customer with options shows that you're engaged and dialed into their needs.

Daryl Corbin, Director, TIBCO Professional Services Group

152 Understanding Partner Conflict

Anyone who has been involved with the PS organization in a quarterly driven enterprise software company knows the issue. The PS team is being held to specific revenue targets. Yet, the software sales team understands the leverage that partners bring to the table. But, in return the partners want the services revenue. Herein lays the conflict between the partner channel and the services team. In my opinion, the problem arises because the two organizations have a very different view of what constitutes an effective partner. For sales, it is partners that drive leads and new software business. For PS, it is partners that are capable of delivering quality deployments and working with the PS organization in a blended team concept. So how can an organization make this work?

There are obviously many different strategies employed to create effective, collaborative partnerships, but they all have to start with the basics. An organization must have a firm understanding of why they are partnering in the first place. If the goal of developing partners is to drive distribution and distribution reach, the organization must define a partner profile that reflects a partner's ability to sell and deliver solutions. The PS team needs to be part of that process and understand the importance of those partnerships. If the partners that end up as part of the program do not fit the bill, then they need to be moved to a part of the program that caters to their abilities. This needs to be constantly re-visited and corrections made as needed.

Recruit the right partners in the first place.

As an example: The sales team wanted to leverage the partner community to drive more license sales, yet upon investigation, we found that most of the partners that the sales team had engaged were not truly capable of driving new license transactions. They had almost no sales capability and were not properly trained to effectively represent the product. They were primarily capable of services fulfillment and were minimally helpful in providing leverage for the actual software sales transaction. This is also where the PS team had the biggest conflict. In the opinion of the PS team, the partners were not really helping with the sales transactions and were essentially competing for the implementation and follow-on services opportunity. Sound familiar? And guess what, the partners weren't happy in this relationship either.

By setting proper expectations internally as well as externally with partners, an organization at least will have a shot at success. Without Partner, Sales and PS alignment, the desired sales leverage and service teaming cannot occur.

Mark R. Williams, Management Consultant

153 Building a System Integrator Channel

For companies with relatively young products and a relatively short history of delivering implementation services, building an SI channel can be a significant challenge. There are two major motivations for building the channel: 1) to increase delivery capacity and 2) to broaden penetration by developing an indirect sales channel. For young companies, the more typical motivator is to extend sales penetration by working through partners who already have a customer base that relies on their services. The question becomes: what can you offer these partners to entice them to bring you into their established customers?

While the obvious first incentive is to provide partners with some margin, most integrators prefer to maintain product independence, making margins on license revenue problematic. This is especially the case for young product companies that are only beginning to gain market share. What integrators are looking for is fairly different from what you, as a service organization within a product company, find important. License revenue is not important, but successful, predictable implementations are necessary. And, obviously, you need to find partners whose business is complementary, in the sense that you can provide them avenues to grow revenue within existing clients and by extending their client base.

Increase delivery capacity and broaden penetration by developing an indirect sales channel.

To make the channel effective, there are a slew of issues to address, but top of the stack would be:

- Keep the list short. You will need to be bringing opportunities to your partners, likely before they will introduce you to their established clientele. There is no point in bringing on more partners than your sales group can seed.
- Don't ask the partner to dedicate resources to training on your product without a customer deal signed. Good SIs don't have deep benches and training time is expensive.

- Take the risk out of the early engagements. Go in side-by-side to provide OTJ training (likely in addition to classroom training spurred by an engagement) for the partner's consultants with your team taking all the risks.
- Align the sales teams and minimize compensation conflicts. You need your sales team to work well with the integrator which means they cannot be penalized for services delivered via a partner rather than through in-house services.
- Take the lead on marketing. This is not usually a strength of the smaller integrators.
- Provide an implementation methodology. You need to do everything possible to ensure that the partner is successful and profitable, even on the early engagements.

The commitment of the organization as a whole is required to successfully launch a partner channel. But once established, the channel can greatly accelerate market penetration for young product companies.

Neil Blumenfield, VP, Professional Services, Fortify Software

154 Stakeholders in a Partner Strategy

When determining Partner Strategy, be sure to understand the points of view of all major stakeholders within your firm and the partner firm in order to gain congruence and the most optimal arrangement for all.

Below is an example slide I have used in getting two software companies I have worked for to understand the different viewpoints which need to be addressed:

What Key Stakeholders Seek in Partnering

Executive Management

– Partner firms who endorse our company's solution and help grow the overall market.

When determining partner strategy, be sure to understand the points of view of all major stakeholders.

Sales – Partner firms that can help shape larger deals, close deals faster and create referenceable customers.

Alliances – Partner firms that can bring new leads and spread the word about our company's solution.

PS Delivery – Partner resources who can deliver projects at high quality, and who need minimal assistance on their own sold projects. Leverage key partners for alternative delivery models.

Partner Firms – Significant services fees for consulting projects involving our company's technology, preferably on their contract paper. Enablement (training, mentoring, best practices), preferably free of charge, from our company.

Thomas Murphy, VP Professional Services, Integrien Corporation

155 One Way to Reduce Channel Conflict with Partners

All software companies purport to be "partner friendly" and look to partners to provide additional sales and services delivery capability. This approach typically puts an internal services team in direct conflict with partners for services revenue. One method for overcoming that challenge is to have the internal services team focus on a "packaged services" model where the internal services team focuses on delivering high-value, time-bound services like business-level consulting around a product, product installation and configuration and product upgrade services and cedes the product customization and lower level development tasks to partners. To do this, the services team defines the set of services that require "expert services" and package the delivery of those services. The packaging includes producing datasheets, standardized pricing based on some defined parameters, and allowing the sales team to sell the services on the standard price list. Obviously, this approach requires a highly skilled partner community to do the heavy lifting (aka full implementation) on a project with oversight and review by the internal services team, but does achieve the goal of providing partners with an incentive to recommend a software product and does ease the channel conflict and rate challenges between partners and internal services teams.

Scott Hussey, Director, Business Development, Lombardi Software

156 Forming Alliances

When starting at a new company, or taking responsibility for a new industry or practice group, take out a sheet of paper and write down all the alliances you need to form to be successful. I am not talking about external partnerships, but about internal alliances. In whatever business you are in, you must ultimately rely on and influence others to get the job done. Unless you are the CEO, not all of these colleagues report to you. You must leverage your own influence and topical knowledge to persuade colleagues to assist you in the completion of a deal, organizational restructuring, new venture, or whatever you need to accomplish.

> 🕮 **Identify alliances and build on them.**

Meet with these individuals on a regular basis. If you are in the services group of a software company, you not only need to meet with the license folks with whom you are aligned, but you must also convey your value to them in the deal cycle. Once you become a trusted member of their pursuit team, particularly on large, strategic opportunities, you will find it easier to describe the value of your company's service offerings in the process... direct to the client. Over time, as they gain trust in you, you will become a major asset to them. In fact, you will find that you will become an executive sponsor for significant opportunities on your own. It all starts with alliances you form early on.

Keith Costello, SVP Consulting, SAP

157 You Can Have Too Many Relationships

We started a professional services firm a few years ago with a grand idea that we could be nimble and flexible and work with all kinds of other PS partners. It would be ok for us to partner with a firm in our space because we could leverage their talents when our staff was booked and hopefully they will call us when their resources were fully utilized. It was good for us to "partner" with a group overseas to offer our customers services at their other global sites. Of course, it made sense to align with a PS firm that provides non-competitive services so we could refer work back and forth to each other.

Between the four partners of the firm, we had countless relationships. We often spent a tremendous amount of time managing these relationships resulting in little or no benefit to what we were trying to do as a firm. When we focused on key relationships and actually worked to make them successful, we achieved success for both our "partners" and for our mutual customers.

Having relationships with other PS firms can be a tremendous benefit in terms of what you can offer your customers and being introduced to new prospects. Having too many relationships can be taxing on the people that need to manage those relationships and prevent you from being successful with any one of them. Make sure you define what you want out of the relationship, how the company you are going to align with can help you (in comparison to other firms) and who will manage the relationship. Otherwise you may end up spending a lot of time with little value to you which makes being successful in a PS business extremely difficult.

> **When we focused on key relationships and worked to make them successful, we achieved success for both our partners and for our mutual customers.**

Tom Keuten, Principal, Pariveda Solutions

158 Managing Partners Using the "80/20 Rule"

The globalization of markets, supply chains, distribution channels, and client demand for total or end-to-end solutions vs. point products is driving the need for companies to explore partnerships more than ever.

Apply the "80/20 Rule" as a model to determine relative fit and synergy of a prospective partner. A simple rule of thumb is that 80% of capabilities should be complementary (not overlap) with a maximum of 20% capabilities overlap between partners. The greater the capabilities overlap (current or future), the higher the likelihood that the partnership will ultimately fail or dissolve. While most partnerships start with good intentions, partnerships that have significant capabilities overlap are difficult to sell internally. These overlapping partnerships are also difficult to sustain long-term due to competing services between the partner companies.

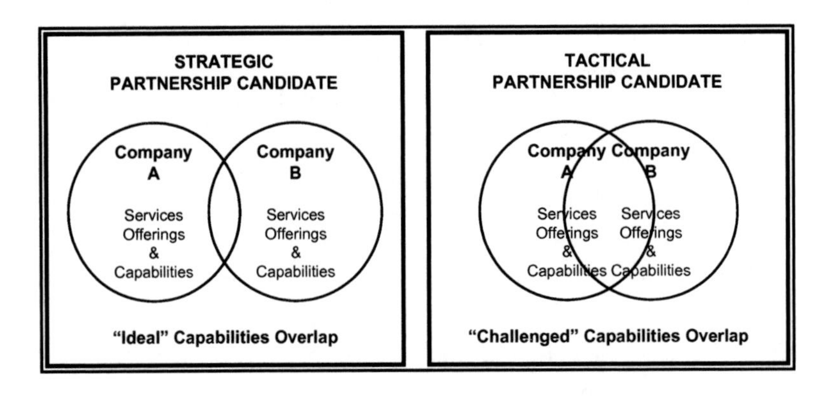

This is not to say that partnerships where there are significant capabilities overlap should not be formed. However, it is essential to recognize the capabilities overlap and develop formal agreements to protect each partner (IP, contracts, client relationships, etc.). It should also be understood that this type of partnership is tactical (i.e., to sell a specific deal) and will likely not be long-lived. Prior to entering this type of partnership the long-term risks should be weighed against potential short-term gains including the potential loss of IP and allowing or enabling market and/or customer entry to a potential competitor.

Finally, whether the partnership is tactical or strategic in nature the following are 10 key success criteria you can use to analyze, establish and manage a successful partnership.

10 Key Partnership Success Criteria

Common Interest – you must have realistic and clearly defined goals and objectives.

Financial Benefits – all roads ultimately lead to money and each partner must continually receive value (revenue and/or profit) from the partnership in order to maintain a sustainable relationship.

Market and Whole Product Value – the value of the combined partnership products or services brings greater market value than that of individual parts.

Synergy – services/products should be complementary and have minimal overlap (current or future); there must be shared organization values and compatible cultures.

Organizational Readiness and Commitment - partner organizations must be both ready and committed to partner with one another.

Communication – there must be strong and fluid communication channels between all levels and geographies of partner organizations and with a unified external message. Clearly defined performance metrics are necessary along with a formal reporting mechanism.

External and Internal Marketing – the partnership, whole product value and market successes must be clearly and continually messaged to both the external market as well as internally to the respective partner organizations.

Walk Before You Run – the partnership should be developed organically with an initial set of successful engagements that enable the whole product to be defined, market value validated, and the operating model built and organizational compatibility determined. Only then can you truly be sure and ready to take the whole product to the market in a big way.

Formal Agreement – clearly articulate and define the partnership agreement.

Focus on the Client – never lose sight of this key construct as it will maintain the right focus and balance of the partnership.

Gerry Leitão, Vice President Professional Services, Compuware

159 Partner Programs That Work

During a time of short staffing due to increased workload, we started our partner program. Here's the process we follow:

Partner Selection and Training: Partners are selected based on reputation, location and technical project implementation experience. A partner then takes a classroom style training class before being paired with a Partner Project Manager. The role of the Partner PM is to be available to answer product implementation questions during implementation.

Contract Assignment: A contract can be assigned to a partner for various reasons:

- Location (close proximity to customer)
- Implementation expertise (partner has implemented similar projects in the past)

Success was achieved through clear definition of roles and responsibilities.

Contract Signing/Partner Acceptance: Contracts are first closed by our sales staff. Once the partner is selected, the contract SOW is reviewed internally to determine what aspects of the contract are to be delivered by the partner. A percentage of the contract hours are retained by the Partner Project Manager to aid in the project implementation. Then the remaining hours are converted to a fixed fee amount less a margin and presented to the partner for approval. The terms of the agreement are 50% up-front paid to the partner and 50% upon completion. All monies are paid to the partner only after being received from the customer. Upon partner approval of the contract, the partner is introduced to the customer.

Customer Kick-off Call & Implementation: The first call to the customer outlines the project deliverables and the process of working with us and a partner. Also addressed on the call are any concerns a customer may have about working with a partner. A key point communicated is that we have the ultimate responsibility with regard to project completion and customer satisfaction. The Partner Project Manager is also involved in regular status calls to monitor progress; this is essential in limiting scope-creep and ensuring that the project stays on track. After a successful implementation the customer is then transferred back to us for on-going support.

John Murphy, VP, Professional Services, Kintera Inc.

160 Sharing Resources Across Lines of Business

As part of a major reorganization, we brought professional services, customer support, and training into one organization. To support resource sharing across the lines of business, we rewarded individual contributors on customer utilization (billable utilization + technical support). While this was a good idea, we did not provide specific guidelines for charging time to customer support. As a result, engineers and project managers, assigned to professional services projects, began charging time to technical support whenever they helped a customer. This ensured high customer utilization and SKEWED headcount planning because Finance rolled up timecard data to calculate full time equivalents (FTEs) for each line of business. Although Finance reported that customer support and professional services were fully staffed, in reality, the hotline was a FEW headcounts short, and professional services were a FEW over capacity.

Managers who share resources must understand how the organization's processes and metrics affect their individual lines of business.

We did not see this problem immediately. It happened over several quarters as we happily reported how well we were doing. We realized this was a problem when we analyzed customer satisfaction issues related to customer support.

The lesson learned is simply that managers who share resources (and the financial analysts who support them) must understand how the organization's processes and metrics affect their individual line of business. And, we need to look beneath the high-level metrics because the devil is always in the details.

Glenda Aune

161 Aligning Business with IT

I often hear clients complain "My IT and business teams are not aligned properly and they don't talk." Top level management always asks the question, "How can I properly align IT with the business to help improve sales and achieve growth?" When the IT department is asked the same question, they say "Business people live in a dream world. They don't understand technology and ask us to do things that are impossible". If this problem really exists how can businesses continue to make money? And what is the real impact?

IT and business can be aligned if you use a solid architectural framework.

Confronted with this IT problem, line-of-business teams often take matters into their own hands. Business personnel create their own small applications to address a particular business problem and load it on a server which can be housed underneath their desk. I call this a "little point business solution".

Since IT is circumvented by user-created solutions, they don't have a clue such an application and infrastructure exists. Little point business solutions can easily cripple the IT support structure and may pose an even greater threat and potential loss to the company itself.

If you flip the coin and draw a parallel of IT departments doing things without consulting the business, equally negative unforeseen consequences can occur. So then how do we align IT with business? Is this even possible? The answer is yes, there are solutions.

One solution is to use a sound architectural framework that integrates business and IT. Why an architectural framework? Architectural frameworks in general usually derive all choices from business and almost always communicate in terms of business benefit. The framework built in such a way doesn't lose sight of the corporate vision which usually drives strategy, and strategy eventually drives architecture. The frameworks also provide a holistic view of business and IT. If adopted properly, it will provide a common mind-set, language and terminology that are understood by both business and IT. Additionally, using the same language helps communicate business and IT impact very easily. To conclude, business and IT can be aligned.

Nirmalraj Yuvaraj, Sr. Manager – IT Architect, Capgemini

162 Develop Key Engineering Contacts

Sometimes implementation of the optimal customer solution – or even an acceptable customer solution – requires extensive field customization. If you have the scope, schedule, and budget to cover the work that can be ok. But I'm probably not the first person who's had accountability for an engagement where it became apparent that the necessary customization work would be more costly and more time-consuming than originally anticipated. Project margins, team morale, and customer relationships can all suffer. On more than one occasion, having the right contacts in our Engineering group helped me out of a jam – the right advice from the right person in Engineering led to a better solution that required far less time to implement (undocumented APIs, hooks that were available, etc.). The first few times I got lucky. One time I happened to be lamenting my problem over lunch with the CTO, and he revealed a way to shave a month off of my project's development effort; another time, my Project Manager similarly happened to go out with a lead Engineering developer who knew about several undocumented (thought reliable and tested!) APIs, again dramatically reducing field customization work. Engineering advice is now something I aggressively seek out whenever faced with a customization challenge. Developing strong relationships with key Engineering contacts gives you invaluable access to information that will make your projects more successful.

Jeff Mueller, Director Professional Services, Skire, Inc.

163 Partnering with Product Management and Engineering

Many of us enjoy the challenges and rewards of building professional services practices in early-stage technology companies (dare I say 'start-ups'). Initially, the relationship between our Product Management and Engineering peers is exciting and collaborative. As everyone goes 'head's down' focusing on the immediate needs we run the risk of falling into a common trap. That is the perception that the Professional Services Organization – your team – addresses a temporary and tactical delivery need.

> 🕮 **What do you do when the PSO has been "marginalized"?**

The organization is considered a necessary evil (cost!) that does not add real value. Professional Services is a stop-gap to keep Engineering out of the field, and will ultimately be reduced to a training function once the product matures. This attitude leads to numerous negative by-products including, but not limited to:

Maturity – Field services are used as a crutch to solve gaps that are never addressed by the product or dismissed as acceptable customizations and/or one-off feature requests

Quality – PS is not considered an internal extension of customers. Consultants are not properly trained or involved in new product roll-outs which may create deep product issues often uncovered by the customer at deployment

Cost – Poor product quality will require more services, re-work and support cycles

The reality, of course, is that an effective services team will be a profit center, building credibility with clients and prospects and adding value across a number of dimensions – including the product lifecycle.

It is important to recognize the pattern of services marginalization before prescribing any corrective action. Here are some early indicators:

P&L – PSO considered a cost center or loss leader

Sales – Deals are closed without PSO input or involvement in estimates

Product Feedback – No formal and accountable feedback channel for PSO into product development for new releases or defect resolution

SIs – Another organization like Product Management owns any system integrator relationships

Garbage Collection – PSO routinely solves Engineering issues for customers and may even be required to maintain 'field patches'

Training – None formally provided; the team uses trial-and-error or must beg, borrow and steal expert input

Kudos – PSO wins, especially client-oriented, are not touted on par with Engineering or Product Management

Here are some suggestions to help shape your remediation strategy:

Create a Plan – At the least, document challenges and identify potential levers

Define Vision – Define the organizational integration vision – near-term, long-term – and challenge it; use trusted advisors and benchmarks

Gap Analysis – Identify gaps between reality and the PSO vision; start working on solutions

Soft-sell Vision – Under the banner of organizational maturity, informally pitch your vision to Engineering, Product Management and other executive stakeholders (vision should be holistic not focused on "problem areas")

Hard-sell Vision – Once sufficient buy-in exists, at the C-level and/or across partner leadership, drive a plan to finalize vision and act with a cross-functional committee

Demonstrated Value – Illustrate how PSO complements other organizations for the greater good: i.e., customer wins, margin and performance gains, product accelerators, consulting tools, domain expertise; ensure Sales team understands and articulates these values

Even senior leaders may need to be educated in PSO 101 to get them "there from here."

Adam Signaigo, WW SOA Solution Executive, IBM Software Group

164 It Pays to Get in Front of Your Customer

Being part of a customer-facing field organization means that you periodically find yourself in difficult customer situations. And the Professional Services team often has the accountability for driving those difficult customer situations to the best possible resolution.Lots of difficult situations can arise: negotiating needed change orders during a difficult phase of a project, fully disclosing functionality limitations and strategizing how to mitigate the impacts, dealing with underperforming PSG staff and potentially negotiating concession hours, etc. Working through difficult issues face-to-face with a customer nearly always leads to a better outcome. A mentor from my early PSG days continually emphasized this, and I believe it more than ever. A colleague of mine once paraphrased, "It's easier for a customer to yell at you and be mad over the phone than in person. So go be there in person!" I've found that being in front of the customer at key points in time results in happier customers, less concession time, more support renewals, and more lucrative SOWs - it pays to get in front of your customer!

> 🕮 **Working through difficult issues face-to-face with a customer nearly always leads to a better outcome.**

Jeff Mueller, Director Professional Services, Skire, Inc.

165 Developing Relationships with Alliance Partners

When deciding on whether to develop a relationship with an alliance partner think about whether they would want to be in your space in the long run (and vice versa). If the answer is yes, the relationship will ultimately breakdown. If one partner wants to eventually get into the space of the other partner, the temptation to replicate the other partner's capabilities and methods is just too great.

George Chen, Principal, Strategos

LaVergne, TN USA
23 February 2011
217646LV00002B/301/A